The With

Soccer Mom

Handbook

For and About Real Moms of Real Soccer Kids

By Janet Staihar & Dick Barnes

Sports Barn
Publishing Company
Washington, DC

The Soccer Mom Handbook

By Janet Staihar & Dick Barnes

Published by:

Sports Barn Publishing Company
5335 Wisconsin Avenue NW, Suite 440
Washington, DC 20015

Publisher's Cataloging-in-Publication
(Provided by Quality Books, Inc.)

Staihar, Janet.
    The soccer mom handbook : for and about real moms of real soccer kids / by Janet Staihar & Dick Barnes. -- 1st ed.
    p. cm.
    Preassigned LCCN: 97-92283
    ISBN: 09658875-1-0

    1. Soccer for children.   I. Barnes, Dick (Richard L.), 1938-
II. Title.

GV944.2.S83 1997   796.334'083
                       QBI97-40796

Printed by McNaughton & Gunn, Inc., Saline, Michigan 48176

10 9 8 7 6 5 4 3 2 1

Table of Contents

Foreword

Been There, Still There

At a time when most people my age have redecorated--now that pink Cheerio-type things don't roll under the counter any more and nerf-ball basketball nets aren't scratching paint off closet doors and now that one-time midfielders, goalies, and strikers are car rental agents, house painters, stockbrokers, medical interns, and fathers and mothers themselves--I am still a soccer mom. That's because my adult sons, Greg and Alexi Lalas, are still playing. But even if they weren't, I'd be following the game just as enthusiastically as I do. I was hooked from the beginning, and it's a pleasure to be still a fan, as well as soccer-mom enough that Jan Staihar and Dick Barnes asked me to contribute a few early lines to this wonderful book.

The soccer mom got some gratuitous visibility during the '96 presidential election. It was inane talk, and the connection between voting and soccer was lost on many, probably having to do with an annoying stereotyping of the sport. But contrary to what the politicians were saying, a soccer mom cannot be pegged. Being one has nothing to do with politics. As Staihar and Barnes put it, all it takes is "a kid who plays soccer!" And being an aging one like me is nothing more than a function of time and luck, with a lot of fun in the process, to which this book is testimony.

The Soccer Mom Handbook gives you a good solid background in soccer, combined with laughs and a basic message of common sense, ingredients that will make being a soccer mom one of the best experiences of your parenting. This book with its ready information all in one place makes me wish I could do it all over again. In my day, I can tell you, we were winging it.

One doesn't plan to be a soccer mom, or shouldn't. When it just happens, perspective has a better chance of staying pure. Music gets practiced. Homework gets done. Balance does its thing.

But I did like going to games, still do. Being into writing obscure things, editing strange manuscripts, working hard, I've always loved the diversion of soccer games, the open-air feel, their festive nature. Basically in the early days I didn't know a whole lot about soccer, the penalty kick, the corner, offside, or "offsides," as I called it, being totally unschooled. If I had had just one chapter, such as "What Are These Kids Playing?" (see page 15), I would have graduated from clueless mother to bona fide soccer mom much faster.

The Soccer Mom Handbook has lots of good advice on ways to share your family's interest in soccer, that great connector. I recognize in it many things my boys loved, like going to professional games and college games, reading soccer publications, watching games on television--all things you can do with them. Soccer camps were also a favorite. We didn't have the Internet in those days, but today it's a good source of soccer information for the whole family.

Of course the most valuable thing you can do is attend your children's games. My boys seemed to like that. You're there when they score, make mistakes, when their teams win or lose. They may see you only out of a corner of their eye, or pretend not to see you at all, but you can be sure there's comfort with the knowledge that family is there.

And as much as they want you there, they don't want you to pay *too* much attention to the game. A subtle presence is all it has to be. Believe me, they know who the pushy parents are. Who the criticizers are. Who have the hawk eyes and forked tongues. Kids are completely humiliated when their own parent yells an obscenity or insults them. Hey, own goals happen.

I talked a lot at games. The recipe and hair kind of talk. The wallpaper kind. The dented quarter-panel kind. I've made lots of friends through soccer, met many foreigners, heard many accents, and broadened my knowledge of the world. The global thing about soccer *is* true. I heard about a group of parents once (it seemed there were a lot of Italians among them) who started out on the sideline every Saturday until the opera came on. Then they all gathered around a radio under a tree, sort of a "Three Tenors" type crowd, with one eye on the dial, the other on the game. Now that's culture for you.

One of *our* coaches, who used a rather curious English as a Second Language, coined my favorite expression: "Size the day, boys, size the day!"

The Soccer Mom Handbook will help you do exactly that. Enjoy yourself.

Anne H. Woodworth

"I don't understand it. They all run up, they all run down. I don't know who is play-ing what. And what is offsides?"

--Two-time Oscar winner Meryl Streep, mother of four youth league soccer players, quoted in *People* magazine

A Handbook for
Soccer Moms

"Soccer Mom."

She's a recent find for political pollsters and pundits, but mass market advertisers have realized for several years that soccer is now the across-the-board sport of American youth.

Boys, girls, 6-year-olds, 12-year-olds, 19-year-olds all are playing the world's most popular sport, but one that had grown quietly in the sports shadows of the United States until exploding to broad recognition in 1994.

Now the players – and their Moms – are in the spot-light. Reporters, columnists and talking heads have specu-lated ad nauseam and to no consensus about how to define Soccer Moms politically and sociologically. We prefer the definition of political consultant Todd Domke, quoted in *The Palm Beach Post*:

"They're just moms who go to soccer games."

Some Soccer Moms run leagues or clubs or teams. Others just haul kids and watch from the sidelines, some a bit befuddled about the game like Meryl Streep, some won-dering what's in soccer for their kids. All it takes to be a Soccer Mom is a kid who plays soccer!

The Soccer Mom Handbook will help you understand and appreciate the game. It will give you information and tips so you can support your player in getting the most out of soccer. You'll find plenty of laughs along the way. And we'll tell you what offside is!

This handbook is organized so that you don't have to read straight through from front to back to find the information you most want. Just check the section titles and subtitles in the table of contents and jump to what you're looking for. For example, if you're driving to an out-of-town tournament later this week, you may want to turn right away to "On the Road", the section on page 103 about off-field tactics that can improve the on-field play of a team away from home for the weekend. Or, if your player is starring in her first season on a select first division team, you may be most interested in turning to page 113 to check out her possible future soccer opportunities as discussed in "Wow! My Kid Really IS a Good Player!"

Whether you read *The Soccer Mom Handbook* straight through, in your own purposeful order, or randomly, we want its information to enhance your player's soccer and your enjoyment of being a Soccer Mom, and the funny stuff to make it all more bearable when you're cold and drenched, driving your overcrowded, overtrashed car home from a bad loss.

Acknowledgements

We have met soccer moms, dads, coaches, officials, administrators, journalists and players across the country. They collectively all contributed in one way or another to *The Soccer Mom Handbook*, for which we thank them.

Special thanks go to Anne H. Woodworth, who wrote the foreword, and to our peer reviewers, Joy Mele and Jan Schoenbauer. They each spotted flaws and offered valuable help on everything from broad concepts to typos.

Blame only the authors, however, for any errors or for anything you just plain dislike or with which you don't agree.

"Today's soccer moms are in the driver's seat in many ways, driving the kids, the family, the values, the country. Rushing to soccer, to ballet, to piano lessons, to market, they are '50s women with a difference. Many have chosen this busy, focused, home-based life, after having had busy, focused careers away from home. Smart, aggressive, they've left the office and now run home as if it were business. There are also, of course, plenty of soccer moms with full-time office jobs and major home jobs too. They're the ones whose Dodge vans always need a washing."

--Susan Stamberg
National Public Radio, Weekend Edition

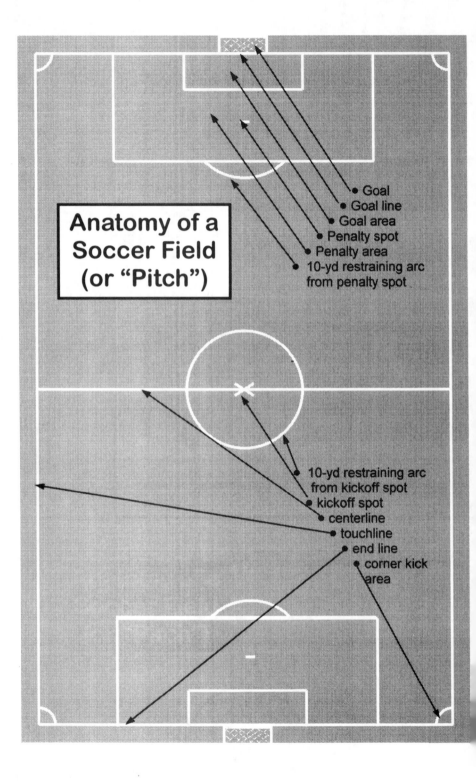

Anatomy of a Soccer Field (or "Pitch")

- Goal
- Goal line
- Goal area
- Penalty spot
- Penalty area
- 10-yd restraining arc from penalty spot
- 10-yd restraining arc from kickoff spot
- kickoff spot
- centerline
- touchline
- end line
- corner kick area

What are These Kids Playing?

A brief introduction to soccer
for the absolute novice spectator

Object of the game

Soccer is one of those games, like football, basketball, field hockey and lacrosse, whose object is to put the ball into a goal area at the opponents' end of a rectangular playing surface. Each such accomplishment in soccer is called a goal, and each goal counts as one. The team that puts the ball into its opponent's goal the most times wins. Proper verbal terminology for a final score is, for example, three-two, or three goals (never "points") to two. Soccer is perhaps the most difficult sport in which to score, so scoreless ties and 1-0 games are not unusual.

The field and the ball

Soccer is played on a grass field 100 to 120 yards long and 50 to 80 yards wide. (An American football field, including the end zones, is 120 x 53 yards.) Soccer people with a background in England often refer to the playing surface as the "pitch". At the middle of each endline is a goal 8 feet high and 24 feet wide with a net flowing out behind it. The field is marked with four boxes, a circle and six arcs as shown on the diagram to the left. A triangular flag on a small pole is usually at each corner of the field. The soccer ball is round, inflated, made of leather or a synthetic, and is slightly smaller than a basketball. The ball's stitched surface enables players to make kicks that curve substantially.

The Players

There are 11 players on the field at one time for each team in a full-sized game. One is the goalie, whose job is to defend the goal against any ball that gets past the goalie's teammates. Only the goalie can put hands or arms on the ball, and then only within a prescribed area. The other 10, the field players, may move the ball about the field by kicking it, knocking it with the head, or having it bounce off other body parts except for the hands or arms.

There is no required player formation in soccer. Most teams will use three to five of their field players in defensive positions nearest their own goal, four to six players in the midfield, and one to three as the principal attackers of the opponent's goal. Formations often are referred to by the number of defenders, midfielders and forwards (for

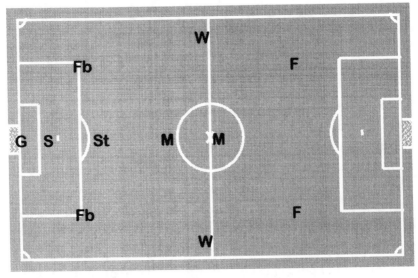

One typical formation, the 4-4-2

G - Goalie
S - Sweeper
Fb - Fullback
St - Stopper

W - Wing
M - Midfielder

F - Forward

example, 4-4-2; the goalie is not included in the count). Defensive positions are typically called sweeper, fullback and stopper. Midfield positions most often are called midfielder and wing. An attacker is usually called a forward or a striker. Positions are very fluid, so defenders may sometimes be on the attack, and attackers may sometimes drop deep into the defense.

Depending on the age level and applicable rules, teams usually will have up to seven substitutes available. They may enter the game only during certain stoppages in play.

Scoring

Scoring a goal most typically occurs when the attacking team passes the ball quickly among 2-4 players and one of them gets free for a shot on goal before the goalie can fully adjust. Passes back and forth across the field often can draw the goalie out of position. Sometimes an individual attacker will score by dribbling (controlling the ball with a series of short kicks as he runs) and faking his way through or around the defenders and then shooting past the goalie.

Out of bounds

The in-bounds/out-of-bounds distinction in soccer is different from other major American sports. To be out of bounds, the entire ball (not just any portion touching the ground) must be over the entire line. A player out of bounds touching a ball in bounds does not make the ball out of bounds. The ball may be ruled out of bounds while in the air even if it curves back in bounds before hitting the ground.

If the ball goes out of bounds along the sideline, or touchline, the team that did not last touch the ball before it went out gets to throw it back into play, using a restric-

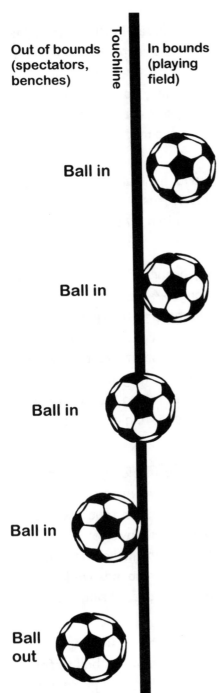

**Out of bounds
(spectators,
benches)**

**In bounds
(playing
field)**

Ball in

Ball in

Ball in

Ball in

**Ball
out**

tive type of throw in-
tended to keep the ball
from going too far. This
is the one case where a
field player, who is actually off the field for the
throw-in, can use her
hands. Both hands must
propel the ball from be-
hind the player's head
while both feet are on
the ground. The ball also
must be thrown—it can-
not just be dropped.

If the ball goes over
the end line off an at-
tacking player, the de-
fending team puts the
ball back into play with a
free kick from a front
corner of its goal area.

If the ball goes over
the end line off a de-
fender, the attacking
team puts the ball back
into play with a free kick
from the nearest corner
of the field. This is
called a corner kick, and
often gives the attacking
team an excellent oppor-
tunity to score because

the kick can be delivered into a cluster of players in front of the opponent's goal.

Officials

Soccer is officiated by a referee on the field and two assistant referees (sometimes called linesmen). The assistants each move along one sideline between midfield and the endline to their respective right as they face the field. The referee times the game, calls fouls, determines if a goal has been scored and is in complete charge of the game once it begins. The assistants determine (subject to overruling by the referee) which team gets the throw-in after a ball goes over the touchline, help the referee determine whether a ball over the endline should result in a goal kick or a corner kick, and signal the referee if an offside violation or a foul has been committed.

Offside

Offside is the most difficult rule in soccer both to observe and to interpret. Purpose of this rule is to prevent a team from stationing its attackers right in front of the opponent's goal to wait for long passes. The rule requires that if an attacking player is closer to the goal than the ball at the time the ball is played toward the goal by a teammate, then at least two players on the defending team (one of whom is usually the goalie) must be as close, or closer, to the goal as is the attacker. Closeness is determined by perpendicular distance to the end line.

The rule is difficult to observe because it is hard for an official (or a spectator) to simultaneously watch the ball being kicked, and the relevant attackers and defenders, who may be 30 or 40 yards closer to the goal. After the ball has been kicked, a fast attacker in pursuit of the ball

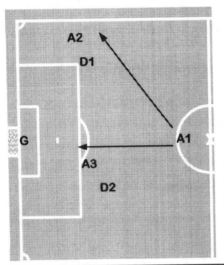

Figure 1 - Players as positioned at moment ball is kicked. If A1 passes to A2, offside should be called because only the goalie is between A2 and the goal, as measured perpendicular to the end line; this is true even if A2 comes upfield of D1 to field the pass. If A1 passes to A3, offside might not be called; A3 is onside because he is no closer to the goal than the goalie and D1, and A2, though in an offside position, may be considered no factor in the play if he does not run toward the ball.

In diagrams, players labeled "A" are attackers, "D" are defenders, "G" is goalie

Figure 2 - Players as positioned at moment corner kick from A1 is headed by A2 to A3. Offside should be called because A3 is closer to the goal than every defender. Had the header gone to A4, the referee would have to decide whether A3 was a factor in the play or not; A4 is not offside because he is not closer to the goal than D1, D2 or the goalie. Had the corner kick gone directly to A3 (assuming the same positions at the time of the kick), there would have been no offside; there can't be offside on a corner kick, since the ball is at the end line. On corner kicks, the goalie often moves off the goal line to try to catch the ball, further complicating the task of determining whether two other defenders are closer to the goal than any attacker in the play after the first contact.

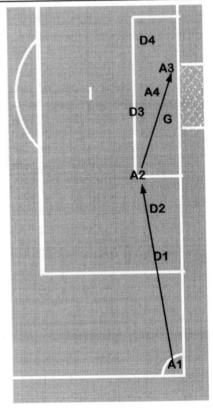

may well get behind all the defenders except the goalie. Spectators rooting for the defenders often will yell "offside, offside." But if the attacker was not behind the next-to-last defender when the ball was kicked, he was not offside.

An assistant referee is supposed to always stay even with the next-to-last defender so as to be in the best position to determine offside. But if play is fast, officials are not always in position for the most accurate line of sight (perpendicular from the sideline) to determine if the attacker is impermissibly ahead of a defender.

A further complication is a risky strategy called the offside trap in which all of the defenders except the goalie suddenly rush upfield in an effort to trap an attacker in an offside position as the ball is about to be kicked by the attacker's teammate.

The offside rule has limited exceptions:

- a violation won't be whistled if the attacker isn't involved in the play even though he is in an offside position.

- there is no offside on a throw-in or a corner kick; however, as soon as the ball is touched by any player, the offside rule is in effect.

- if an attacking player was in the half of the field his team is defending when the ball was kicked, he cannot be offside even if he is behind all of the defenders; this rule generally forces a team to keep at least one defender no further forward than the midfield line.

As an example of the rule's complexity, the official rulebook published by soccer's international governing body includes 21 separate diagrams illustrating various situations in which offside should or should not be called. If you just understand the main principles, you'll be ahead of most of the sideline crowd.

Fouls

Players are allowed to run alongside an opponent and force him off the ball by applying shoulder and hip strength. But elbowing, tripping and grabbing are not allowed. However, many fouls, especially away from the ball, are not seen. Look at attackers away from the ball and you'll sometimes catch a defender grabbing the attacker's shirt to keep him within reach. The referee also may ignore an infraction if the fouled team continues to hold the advantage in the play despite the foul.

A common play that sometimes results in a foul is called a tackle. This is not like a tackle in American football. A slide tackle in soccer occurs when a defending player tries to get the ball away from an opponent by falling to the ground lengthwise on his side and swinging a foot parallel to, and just off, the ground. If the defender's foot knocks the ball away, a foul usually will not be called, even if the opponent trips. But if the defender misses the ball and the opponent is tripped, a foul almost always will be called. Chances of a foul being called increase markedly if the defender is approaching from the rear rather than the side.

The usual remedy for a foul is a free kick by the fouled team (not necessarily the player fouled) from the point of the foul. Depending on the location and nature of the foul, the free kick may be either "direct" or "indirect." The kicker can boot a direct free kick into the goal for a score.

A goal cannot be scored with an indirect free kick until some other player touches the ball after it has been kicked. If a free kick is indirect, the referee will signal direction and keep her arm raised until the ball is kicked. If the kick is direct, the referee will only signal direction.

If a foul is serious or intentional, the referee may show a yellow card to the violator. This is a warning. If a player gets a second yellow card during the game, he is thrown out of the game, and his team must play with one less player ("play short"). The referee can expel a player immediately by showing him a red card for a blatant foul or for fighting. Yellow or red cards also can be shown for verbal criticism of the official, and for certain other technical violations. The referee can warn or expel the coach from the sidelines for impermissible conduct (usually verbal), and in some youth leagues can sanction the coach for bad conduct by the team's parents or supporters.

If an attacking player threatening to score is fouled in the penalty area, the referee may award a penalty kick. A member of the attacking team (not necessarily the player fouled) gets a free kick at the goal from 12 yards out, with only the goalie able to defend. Most penalty kicks are made.

Timing a game

A full-length soccer game lasts for 90 minutes, divided into 45-minute halves. Normally, the referee keeps time with a watch on the field. (Games in Major League Soccer, the top U.S. professional league, and at most colleges are timed on a scoreboard.) The clock does not stop for balls out of bounds, free kicks or other stoppages in play. However, the referee may add additional time to the half if injuries occurred or he thinks one team is unfairly stalling such as by kicking the ball far out of bounds.

Ties

In most leagues and in the round-robin portion of tournaments, soccer games can end in a tie. In tournament games where the winner advances and the loser is out, games normally go to overtime. Lengths of overtime vary, but in most leagues and tournaments, the full overtime is played even if one team scores. Occasionally, sudden death overtime is used, meaning that the game is over if a team scores.

If a game is still tied after the prescribed overtime, the issue usually is settled by penalty kicks. Shooting alternately, each team takes five penalty kicks. The team that makes the greater number wins. If still tied, the teams will continue kicking in rounds of one kick per team until one team is ahead after a round. Only the players who were on the field at the conclusion of the overtime can participate in penalty kicks, and no player can take a second kick until every player on her team has kicked once.

Major League Soccer has a slightly different tiebreaker called the shoot-out. Instead of taking a penalty shot, the shooter dribbles toward the goalie from 35 yards out and must shoot within five seconds. The scoring and sequence of shooting is the same as with penalty kicks.

Rules variations for youths

Youth games have some rules variations:

- Games are shorter: for example, 25-minute halves are typical for 10-year-olds, and 35-minute halves are normal for 13-year-olds.

- Free substitution is usually permitted during certain stoppages in play; in international adult soccer, substitutions are very limited, and a player who has left the game for a substitute cannot return (however, a player can go off the field to tend to an injury and then return as long as he has not been replaced).

- Pre-teens play with a smaller ball.

- At ages below ten, smaller teams play on smaller fields with smaller goals. The youngest players often play four to a side with no goalie, working up to seven or eight to a side by the time players are in the under-10 age group. The offside rule is not used at the youngest ages or in four-on-four games.

Soccer Mom Juggling Act

" . . . real Americans out there with real problems -- whether soccer moms or . . . whoever it may be."
--Bob Dole, 1996 presidential candidate
second debate with President Clinton

"harried, frazzled, overburdened (but still game and cheerful) women"
--Columnist Molly Ivins
quoted in *Sacramento Bee*

"And they're busy. Sometimes the only chance they have to meet friends is at their kids' -- or their own -- soccer games."
Wisconsin State Journal

"What they share most is that they're exhausted."
--Susan Carroll, Center for American Women and Politics, Rutgers
quoted in *Hartford Courant*

"'Financially stressed' suburban women who try to balance the demands of work and children."
[London] *Daily Telegraph*

"Theoretically, it's possible to be a soccer mom even if nobody in the household plays soccer, so long as you're sufficiently stressed out."
Kansas City Star

26

Practices aren't at 4 a.m.

Top ten reasons why soccer is a great sport for kids -- from a Mom's perspective

10 Less equipment to buy than for nearly all other sports except swimming, and it can be played almost anywhere in some form or another.

9 A fast ball to the forehead won't leave a bump that looks like a walnut, unlike baseball; in fact, heading the ball is part of the game.

8 Opportunities are generally equal for girls and boys from younger ages (where they often play together) on through high school, college and even to the Olympics and national team level.

7 The basic game is simple enough to play successfully at age 5 or 6, and provides young kids continuous exercise rather than mostly standing around.

6 Games are a predictable length.

5 Performance results are not totally judge-based, unlike gymnastics, diving or figure skating.

4 Cross-culture exposure—kids from other countries now in the U.S. are more likely to play soccer than other sports, and many coaches are from other countries.

3 Everyone on the field gets frequent opportunities with the ball.

2 Kids don't have to be extremes of nature to succeed at the higher levels, unlike basketball centers or football linemen.

1 The practices don't start at 4 a.m., unlike some ice rink practice times for hockey and figure skating.

How Many Kids Play Soccer?

▷ More than 3 million boys and girls under 19 now register to play soccer with U.S. club teams.

▷ The number of registered U.S. youth players has more than tripled since 1980.

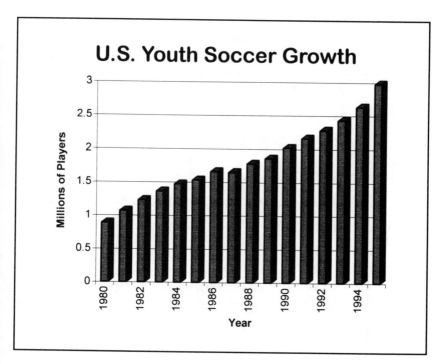

U.S. Youth Soccer Growth

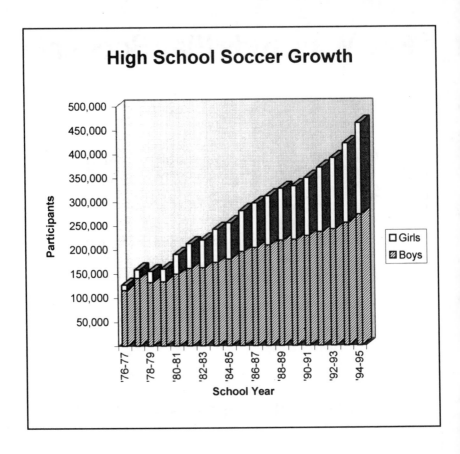

High School Soccer Growth

Participants (y-axis): 50,000 — 500,000

School Year (x-axis): '76-77 ... '94-95

Legend: ☐ Girls ▨ Boys

▷ More than 460,000 soccer players now compete on U.S. high school teams.

▷ More than 40 per cent of high school soccer players are girls.

▷ Seven times as many girls and twice as many boys are playing high school soccer now as compared to 1980.

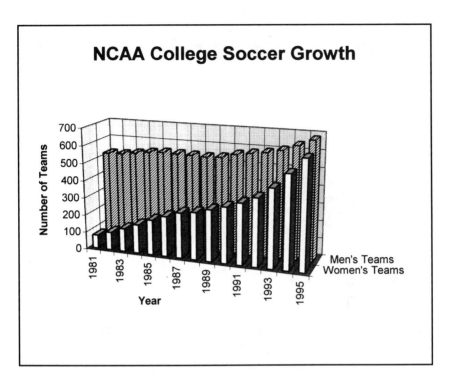

NCAA College Soccer Growth

Number of Teams / Year

Men's Teams
Women's Teams

▷ Eight times as many NCAA colleges now have a women's soccer team as had one 15 years ago.

▷ Soccer is the second-leading participant sport for U.S. youths under 12, trailing only basketball.

▷ Soccer is the third-leading participant sport for U.S. youths under 18, trailing only basketball and volleyball.

--All figures from Soccer Industry Council of America data

Soccer Mom Self Portraits - I

"Being a soccer mom means standing in wet grass at 7 a.m. on Saturday mornings, drinking cold coffee on the sidelines. It means weekend treks to places like Birmingham and Jackson, and checking in at midnight on Friday at the local Shoney's Inn. It means a minivan that smells like a locker room and a refrigerator full of 10K, all flavors. It means filling up my car with gas (regular, self serve) three times a week."

--Renee Peck, Louisiana

By-line article in *The* [New Orleans] *Times-Picayune*

Yells and Screams
from the Parent Sideline

 Good effort, Joe. Next time!

 Joe! You choke on that shot every time!

 Encourage, don't demean.

 Way to bounce back up, Susan!

 Don't take that, Susan; knock her down!

 Don't promote retaliation.

You got her, Ashley; keep it up!

 Don't let her fake you out this time, Ashley!

 Show optimism, not pessimism.

Offside. sir! [only if you under-stand the offside rule]

 Wake up! He was a mile offside!

 Everybody yells at the ref a bit. Keep it respectful, matter-of-fact and impersonal.

 Don't worry about it, Kevin; we'll get it back!

 Cheap goal, Kevin; hold onto the ball next time!

 Goalies distracted by a bad play often make another one soon af-ter. Don't feed the distraction.

Super playing, Brenda!

 Aw, Jeez, coach, don't take her out now!

 If you question coaching tactics, do it in private with the coach off the field.

 Don't let him bother you, Tris!

 Hey, number 4, you're a thug; clean it up!

 Don't yell or talk to opposing players. (Post-game compliments are okay, but parking lot arguments are not.)

Way to attack, Kim!

 Kim! Next time down, take it in-side and then dump it out to the corner for Tiffany!

 Leave the field tactics to the coach.

 C'mon, guys, just play soccer!

 Hey, buddy, you pay your coach to teach your kids that garbage?

 Don't get in arguments or shout-ing matches with the other team's parents.

 Play splendidly and emerge tri-umphant!

 Pound the b-st-rds and win the #@&*ing game!

 Watch your language. There are kids around and you're in public.

Soccer Mom Self Portraits - II

"Hooray for soccer moms. I'm the soccer queen. This is a soccer family. I think it's so wonderful that I get to run around on soccer fields with some of the brightest young people we have. The joie de vivre associated with soccer, I don't see anywhere else. It's almost spiritual."

--Stacy Kalstrom, California
quoted in *Sacramento Bee*

New Educational and Career Opportunities

Soccer offers Mom a broad array of opportunities to enhance her education and gain experience for new careers such as these.

Meteorologist

You've never been truly wet and cold until you've stood on a muddy sideline through an entire soccer game in a downpour in the late fall.

You've never been truly hot and exhausted until you've stood through an entire cloudless day of tournament games at a treeless field complex with the temperature over 100°--and you forgot your hat.

Soccer is played in all kinds of weather except lightning storms. Soccer Mom should know how to predict the weather in order to plan what to take to the game—or even whether to expect to go at all. However, bad weather a day or two earlier can result in a postponement even when game day is clear and sunny. That happens because some fields drain poorly, become saturated, take days to dry out sufficiently, and have owners that are quick to close them down.

Medic

Soccer Mom's greatest re-
straint is required not when a referee's outrageous call goes against
her child, but when her player
suddenly crumples to the turf
from an injury during a game.
Kicked ankles, leg bruises
from trips, and bangs from
flying elbows are the most
common soccer injuries. A
hard-kicked soccer ball
into the stomach or groin
can knock a player down,
and two players simulta-
neously attempting a
header who smack heads instead of the ball are likely to
see stars for a bit.

Moms are not supposed
to rush onto the field for in-
juries, especially as players get older. But Moms usually bear the burden of care for minor soccer injuries
and other ailments such as blisters from new shoes or
poison ivy from chasing the ball into those shiny weeds
behind the practice field goal area.

(*See* Doctor Mom, p. 99.)

Psychologist

Soccer can be frustrating for the players. Hardly any shots in a game go into the goal. Any lapse of concentration can cause the ball to be miskicked or even whiffed entirely. Mistakes by the goalie often give the other team a goal. Referees and their assistants some-times make bad calls. Most youth games are played on imper-fect fields that yield crazy bounces, rough footing, poor lighting and other impedi-ments to good play. Play-ers be-come fo-cused on beliefs that a certain teammate won't pass to them, or that they're not starting because the coach dis-likes them. Enter Soccer Mom, the psychologist, to main-tain or re-build her player's confidence while not undermining the authority of the coach, building generic disrespect for officials, or sowing seeds of team disunity.

THE FOUR BASIC FOOD GROUPS
MOM'S VERSION

THE FOUR BASIC FOOD GROUPS
PLAYER'S VERSION

FRIES

Soccer players sprint, run, jog and walk for up to 45 minutes without a break. That means food and fluid intake is important in both the positive sense of fueling performance and the negative sense of avoiding puking on the field.

Soccer Mom has ample quantities and varieties of pasta available for pre-game meals. She buys sports drinks by the case and makes sure her player takes a quart or two along to each game and practice.

Fashion Consultant

Soccer clothing can be used for other sports and recreational wear. That's fortunate, because your player will accumulate an amazing number of soccer shirts and shorts. Recreational teams will issue a new shirt every season. Club teams will have two or three sets of uniforms. Players will try to buy T-shirts or sweatshirts emblematic of every tournament they attend. The catalogs from the major soccer suppliers and mail order houses will be scrutinized in agonizing detail.

And then there are the shoes. Soccer shoes for the young beginner may cost $15 to $30 and might actually last through both seasons of the year before they're

outgrown. But as a player gets better and older, the focus rather quickly shifts to real leather and then exotic leathers, and the prices climb to the $60-$140 range. By high school, coaches are advising players to have two types of shoes— one with molded cleats for hard fields and the other with screw-in cleats for soft or muddy fields. Of course there are also the flat-soled shoes for winter indoor soccer. Because players aren't just running in the shoes, they're kicking as well, the shoes wear out rather quickly.

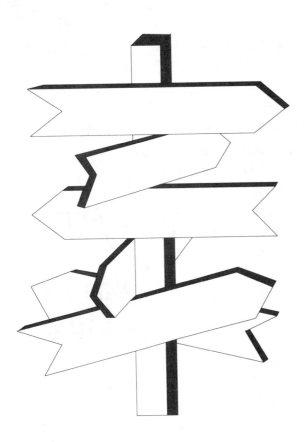

Geographer

    Not all soccer fields are located at your neighborhood school grounds. Some are in industrial parks. Some, especially at tournaments, are temporarily laid out on broad flat areas that are otherwise anything from military parade grounds to polo fields. Some are waaaaay out in the country. A frustrating hunt through farm lands for her daughter's practice field caused comic pages mom Sally Forth to complain in a 1993 strip: "I tell you, if I ever run into the yahoo in charge of putting soccer fields in impossible-to-find places, I'm going to . . ."

Soccer Mom should have at hand a complete set of detailed and current street maps of the region in which her child's games are played. Get them from the auto club or bookstore. Review any written or oral directions to a field against a map of the area. You will be amazed at how many times --

⇒ directions are fine if you are coming from, say, the east, but are useless if you are coming from the west.

⇒ cross streets have one name if you turn right and another name if you turn left; directions may tell you to turn right but use the street name that applies only if you turn left.

⇒ in rapidly developing areas, roads are relocated, cut off by new highways, or have their names changed, making the directions somewhere between confusing and useless; these changes typically happen the week before your game (*see* Murphy's Laws of Youth Soccer, p. 47).

⇒ landmarks change: the Chevron station was bought out by Exxon; the former elementary school is now a job training center; the hamburger stand became a Starbucks.

⇒ the person providing the directions is a total idiot.

What does Soccer Mom do?

"They schedule much of their lives around soccer games and practices. They never miss a game if they can help it, and they encourage their kids by their presence, enthusiasm and dedication. Meal times revolve around soccer practices as do weekend plans. Often an entire family attends the games. They meet other families and friendships strike up."

The [New Orleans] *Times-Picayune*

"The stereotype goes something like this: She is a white, suburban gal on the go, making the lunches and taking Megan and Brett to school, then picking them up, driving them to piano lessons before the soccer coach blows the first whistle of the day. She also cooks dinner."

The San Francisco Chronicle

"She often drives a sports-utility vehicle or a minivan, carries snacks and orange juice for the kids, sometimes takes along extra lawn chairs."

William Safire, *International Herald Tribune*

46

> **Murphy's Law:**
> **If something can go wrong, it will.**

Murphy's Laws
of Youth Soccer

⚽ Major highway repair projects, openings of new roads and other route-changing events always begin the week before, not the week after, your game at an unfamiliar location.

⚽ At least one player on each team will sign their registration card using a different version of their name from that already printed on the card by a parent or team manager.

⚽ The colder the weather, the earlier the kickoff time for your first game at a tournament.

⚽ The earlier the kickoff time for your first game at a tournament, the more distant the field is located from the team hotel.

⚽ The longer your players or parents spend selecting the just-right uniform, the more likely that it will be either on back order or discontinued by the manufacturer.

The more expensive the soccer ball you give your player, the more likely it will end up on the roof of the school next to the field, or lost in the woods behind the goal.

Unless carefully instructed by your player, you will always bring home the wrong flavor of Gatorade from the grocery store.

If your player's high school team has only one Saturday game all season, it will occur on the one weekend your player's club team is in a tournament four hours away.

The only time a Mom leaves abnormally early for a road game is when the game is canceled for an unexpected reason 90 minutes before kickoff and five minutes after she has left home.

The longer the phone tree chain of callers, the more likely the message will be garbled.

Siblings on different teams normally will have practice regularly scheduled at the same time and at fields far apart.

Players who look two or three years bigger and older than your child's age group only play for other teams in your league, never yours.

The more professional experience your team's coach has, the more difficult his accent will be for your players to understand.

The spray paint from a field striper will get on your shoes.

If your team accomplishes something big enough to merit a story in the local newspaper, your player's name will be misspelled.

Any soccer field laid out by someone who is not able to apply the Pythagorean Theorem[1] in practical circumstances[2] will not have square corners.

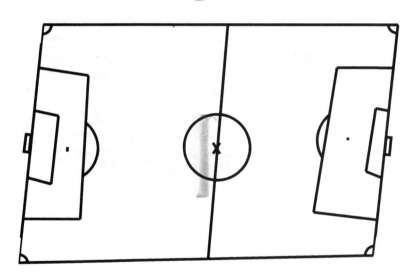

[1]Theorem: the square of the hypotenuse of a right triangle equals the sum of the squares of the two shorter sides of the triangle.

[2]Practice:

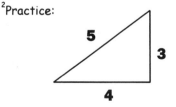

Soccer Mom Self Portraits - III

"Do I define myself as a soccer mom? No. There are lots of other things I'd like to be doing on a Saturday morning, know what I mean? But I guess I am a soccer mom. Acton to Brookline to Foxboro. Travel team, man. Though I usually forget the oranges when I'm supposed to bring them, so maybe I'm not a real soccer mom?"

Perry Allison, Massachusetts
quoted in *The Boston Herald*

Is My Kid Any Good at Soccer?

Moms think their kids are terrific (unless they can't stand them, which is a problem for another venue.)

Soccer Moms think their kids are terrific soccer players, especially when they're young. More accurate appraisals tend to set in after several years, but often still lag reality.

Encouraging a son or daughter who is pretty good at soccer and enjoys it is great.

Pushing a child who is pretty lousy at soccer and doesn't enjoy it is not great.

Usually, the player's ability and interest level will be at least somewhat in synch. The special challenge to Soccer Mom's support are the good players who don't have the interest or aren't having fun, and the poor players who love the sport.

Here are some questions for Soccer Mom to ask herself, her child or the coach in assessing the ability and interest of the kid, especially if she hasn't played the sport herself or hasn't already gone through this with an older sibling.

Ages 5-8

These are the introductory years for young players. In most soccer organizations, the emphasis is on so-called small-sided play: often just four players per team, no goalie, a small field, smaller goals, lots of scoring and plenty of touches of the ball for every player.

- Is the player scared of getting hit by the ball? (Bad sign; try gently kicking the ball around with your child in the back yard; no future in the game if this fear persists.)

- Can she run and jog and walk somewhat continuously without collapsing in a heap? (Soccer is a continuously active sport, somewhat like basketball and unlike baseball or football; if your player is significantly overweight, either soccer will help trim the pounds or he will have trouble keeping up.)

- Is she quick or fast as compared to the other kids? (Quickness is the ability to react or initiate movement as soon as possible; speed is the ability to run fast, especially, for soccer, in spurts of 10 to 40 yards. Quickness is inherent; speed is mostly inherent. Both are major assets in most sports, but especially in soccer.)

- Is he appropriately aggressive? (Does he move to a loose ball? Does he kick the ball hard or just timidly tap it? However, it's not appropriate to be knocking down the other players.)

- Does she kick the soccer ball around the house or yard? (American youth sports today are a highly regimented series of practices, games, clinics and camps. Some casual play alone or with a friend is both a good sign of interest and a way to build basic skills.)

- Is she having fun? Is her exuberance level similar to other activities that she enjoys? (If soccer isn't fun, why not?)

- Does he seem to get along with the coach, or speak well of the coach? (Coaching personalities vary greatly; some personalities don't work with some kids, though it's a good life experience for the kid to give it a complete try.)

- Do the coach, other players, or other parents regard your child as a team leader? (The best players are generally regarded as the team leaders.)

Ages 9-12

By these ages, the players are starting to sort themselves out by ability and interest. Many of the larger soccer organizations continue recreation level play for these ages, but also provide a more competitive opportunity for the better players to play in "select" leagues within the or-

ganization that have designations such as "classic" or "all stars." The best players with a strong interest in the game and a supportive parent or other adult are migrating to "travel" teams that play in area-wide select leagues and tournaments. For levels above all-comers rec leagues, the player and family decide whether to try to step up, but the coach is the one deciding whether your player is selected to the team. Both classic and travel teams are referred to as "select," but the travel teams, on average, are the more competitive.

- Is your player one of the most skillful in her rec league games, or is he particularly strong in at least one major phase of the game? (A player might, for example, be excellent on defense and have a booming kick, but not be much good at dribbling in traffic or scoring goals. Beware of player dominance at this age that is a product mostly of size or advanced growth rather than skills; other players will soon catch up.)

- Is she developing a sense for the game? (The early years of all the players clustering on the ball should be history. Does he understand the responsibilities of his position, but show creativity and create opportunities? Does she talk to teammates during play to advise on threats or opportunities?)

- Have any coaches approached you or your player about trying out for a more competitive team? (Many coaches scout lower level teams to find players for their classic or select teams.)

- Does he show a real interest in soccer? (In this age range, players getting "into" soccer will begin poring over soccer equipment and apparel catalogs, will enjoy going to professional or college games in your area, and may watch some of the increasing amount of soccer on TV.)

- Is your child ready to make the necessary time commitment to travel soccer? (A tournament may conflict with his best friend's birthday party; Sunday games will make it tough for her to always sing with the church choir, and so forth.)

- How does soccer stack up with other sports in her life? (Good athletes at this age can be good in a variety of sports. At this age, enjoying a variety of sports should be encouraged, but at the same time, there is no point in joining both a soccer team and a lacrosse team if they both play all their league games at conflicting times on Sunday afternoons.)

- How much playing time is he getting with his higher-level team? (Most classic or select leagues don't require that each player be on the field for at least half of the game, as is typical in rec leagues. Therefore, playing time serves as an implicit evaluation by the coach. If it's low, the player or parent should ask what can be done to increase it.)

- What did her camp coach report? (By this age, players may be going to either day or sleepover soccer camps. Try to observe for half a day to see how your player stacks up with a different group of kids. Some camps provide written assessments.)

Ages 13 and up

By this age, the interested better players have mostly all moved into classic or select programs. A late-blooming

rec player might move up to classic, or a classic player
might still step up to a travel team, but it would be relatively rare in a strong area for a rec player to jump to
travel at this stage simply because he has missed so much
of the training and more intense competition that goes with
travel team play. Of course, a player competing at his appropriate skill level in a rec program can continue to enjoy
and benefit from soccer. Many rec leagues continue on
through the high school years. For the player who has already moved up, Soccer Mom should continue to ask:

- Do her playing time, the coach's evaluations, and any other credible observations indicate she should be playing at a higher or lower level? (All select is not the same; a player who is marginal on a travel team playing in the league's top division for his age group may do very well in the third or fourth division of the league. Or, a dominating classic player may be able to step in at a fairly high travel team level.)

- Is the coach suitable for the player? (At this age and level, many coaches are paid, unlike the parent volunteers that are typical at younger ages. If most of a team has problems with a coach, the coach likely will be removed. If just one player has a problem, the player will probably have to switch teams to avoid the problem. If a player is good, but doesn't fit the coach's style, look for a better fit with another team.)

- Is soccer his best and favorite sport? (By high school, it becomes increasingly difficult to play at the top level of more than one sport because of time conflicts in season, and camps and conditioning programs out of season.)

- Is he going to play high school soccer? (For travel team players, the answer is almost always "yes," because travel team players typically form the nucleus of high school teams. Depending on the school, players from classic and even rec levels may make varsity or junior varsity teams. Once again, whether she makes the team and then how much she plays will provide an assessment of how good a player she is.)

Soccer Mom Abandons Children in Middle of Car Pool, Cites Need to Get, Have a Life

Submission of Gillian Maness, Fairfax, VA., whose four kids all play travel soccer, to *Washington Post* columnist Bob Levey in response to his call for Headlines the World Needs to See.

--Bob Levey's Washington,
The Washington Post

Talking to the Coach

Talking to the coach about a player is in some ways like talking to the classroom teacher about a student. Some parents are intimidated, and some seek to intimidate; some parents talk too much in one way or another, and some don't ask enough, so they don't get the information they ought to have.

The coach's work is even more visible than the teacher's. Parents generally can't sit through school class-room sessions, but they usually can observe as much soccer practice as they want, and of course can watch the games. Teachers gener-ally have some training in dealing with parents. But coaches may have  none, and will vary widely in how, and how much, they want to communicate with parents. Some coaches will call par-ents and chat at length, even interminably. Others will ex-pect you to initiate any contact, and may not be very re-sponsive. The level of communications also will vary by age and level of play.

Make sure at the outset of a new relationship with a coach to ask his communications preferences. Or, if your team is obtaining a new coach, the screening committee ought to state the team's communications expectations during the interviews.

Here are some general guidelines for communicating with coaches that are appropriate for most situations in which you have a substantive inquiry about your player.

➡ Don't try to start your discussion during practice, or before or during a game (except, of course, for a health emergency such as observing your player in the early stages of an asthma attack). Those are the most intense times for the coach, and she has the entire team, not just your player, to worry about.

➡ A brief inquiry may work okay after a game or practice, but if you want or expect an extended review, just use those times to ask if it's convenient for you to phone that evening.

➡ Keep the discussion civil. You may be calling because you're unhappy, but don't expect yelling to improve your chances of gaining satisfaction.

➡ Focus on getting information or passing on concerns about your child. Don't advise on how soccer should be coached unless you're asked. (If you want to coach, get a team.)

➡ Playing time and playing position are the most frequent causes of parent unhappiness. Rather than starting out by accusing the coach of being unfair to your child or failing to recognize the obvious talents of a striker, just ask why your player is only getting 20 minutes a game or is being used at sweeper.

→ Before talking to the coach, talk to your player to see if he's unhappy about the same thing that is bothering you. Maybe your minds-eye striker prefers to play sweeper, or recognizes that he's the best sweeper even though it's not his favorite position. Maybe your player has already talked to the coach and was satisfied with the answer.

→ Encourage your child to interact with the coach. Depending on the personality of your player, this may involve some pushing. It may help to ask the coach to initiate a conversation with your child. By the time players are in their teens, they should be handling playing time and playing position issues themselves.

→ Try to wrap up difficult discussions on a positive, look-ahead note. Ask what your player should be doing to get more playing time or a chance to play another position. If the coach is telling you that your player is not a good fit for the team, ask for recommendations to other teams.

➡ Don't criticize other players in the course of arguing your player's case. If the coach starts criticizing other players or parents, just interrupt to say that they aren't your concern or responsibility, your player is.

➡ If the conversation doesn't resolve the issue, ask the coach for a follow-up time frame, such as two or four weeks, and then make sure to talk again at that time.

➡ When there is a problem with the coach applicable to the team as a whole, or some group of players, it's generally best to talk to other parents, including the manager, and make a group approach.

➡ Never ever hesitate to interrupt the coach during a game or practice if you see lightning in the near sky.

Soccer Mom Field Kit

Adhesive tape for holding up soccer socks; for holding in place the Band-Aids that keep
coming loose; for covering earrings
that don't come out.

Band-Aids for cuts, scratches, blisters, etc.

Car alarm battery to replace tiny battery in the alarm
activator on your key ring that dies as
you are trying to unlock car to get out
of thunderstorm that has interrupted
game

Cellular telephone for irate call to team manager when
you arrive at the field and no one else
is there; for receiving such calls if
you're the team manager; for finding a
ref when the teams are ready to play,
but no officials have arrived.

Duct tape All-purpose patch and repair item good
for such soccer emergencies as fas-
tening sagging net to crossbar, fixing
shirt torn by grabby opponent (who
didn't even get called for a foul), holding cracked shin guard in stable position on leg, and holding cracked shin in
stable position on temporary splint.

Extra car keys	for use when player accidentally locks regular car keys in the trunk
Folding chair 	unscientific research demonstrates that parents who watch a game from a chair are calmer than those who stand (but then maybe the inherently calmer ones are more likely than the yellers and screamers to bring chairs)
Goal net stakes	they disappear; your coming up with a few extras will win coach or manager's undying gratitude
Ice	soothe sprains and headaches; refresh players on hot day
Inhaler	for asthmatic player
Insect Repellent	for games near woods or swamps
Make-up	(Single moms only) Hey, some of those soccer dads are single, too
Money 	regardless of what time game ends and how recently the last meal was consumed, players are hungry and thirsty
Newspaper	the players have to warm up for 30-40 minutes prior to the game, but what do you have to do?

Scissors	for snipping trendy yarn bracelet from player's wrist after bracelet has shrunk too much to slip off and referee has ordered it removed
Shoelaces	they break as much on soccer boots as on school shoes
Sports watch	for timing game so you don't keep having to ask someone else how much time is left, and so you can answer parents who ask you
Trash bag	16 (or 32) plastic or glass bottles make a mess, not to mention paper plates, wrappers, and so forth
Umbrella	the bigger the better; it's not always 70° and clear

Velcro tape	See Duct tape (same principle)
Yellow card	for flashing at the referee after parents have been told they'll be banned to the parking lot if there is one more word from the sideline

Who is Soccer Mom According to Analysts?

"a suburban woman who raises children and works outside the home."

The Providence Journal-Bulletin

"middle-class women who, between full- and part-time jobs, school and practice, view the world through the lens of their kids."

Morning Star (Wilmington, NC)

MONTH _____

SUN	MON	TUE	WED	THUR	FR	SAT

"They disagree themselves about what constitutes a soccer mom. Some say it is a woman who works full-time in one job, and then rushes home to arrange play dates, make doctor appointments, review home-work. Others argue a soccer mom is someone who stays home and fills her days--quite easily--hauling kids to karate, coaching soccer and the rest."

Los Angeles Times

"Soccer moms of the 1990's were the 'supermoms' of the 1980's. Many of them have kicked off their high heels and replaced them with Keds to watch their kids."

--Kellyanne Fitzpatrick, GOP pollster

quoted in *The New York Times*

66

"Thanks, Coach, for a Great Year"

(even though we went 1-11-2)

Ideas for a meaningful end-of-season gift from the appreciative parents

The Gift	Its Message
Travel Alarm Clock	Don't oversleep a 7:30 a.m. tournament game again.
Soccer Videos	These pro guys can score; why can't we?
Exercise Equipment	Shed that beer gut so you can keep up with the kids at practice.

George Carlin tape

Quit trying to compete with the champ.

ESOL Course at local community college

Perhaps if the kids knew what you were saying . . .

Phone Voice Scrambler

We know your boss is all over you about how many soccer calls come to the office during the workday. We're not going to stop making them, but perhaps this will help.

3-Minute Egg Timer

Keep this by your telephone to use for limiting your interminable responses to parents who call to ask why their kids aren't playing more.

Ear Muffs

Yeah, we know a couple of the dads go overboard during the games criticizing your substitutions and strategy. Try these, at least in cold weather.

Walkman with Beach Boys cassette

See Ear Muffs. Warm weather variant.

Tickets to a film starring (a) Meryl Streep, or (b) Mel Gibson

We don't want to be witnesses in a divorce case. Take (a) wife or girl friend, or (b) husband or boy friend, somewhere to which (a) she, or (b) he, would like to go instead of another soccer game.

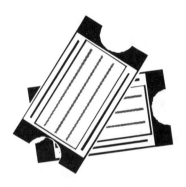

CD: Greatest Hits of The Weavers

This features the all-time favorite, "So Long, It's Been Good to Know You."

Word of the Year

"Soccer Mom" is the choice of the American Dialect Society as Word of the Year.

According to the society's January 1997 press release: "The election is serious, based on members' tracking of new words during the year, but it is far from solemn, since many of the words represent fads and foibles of the year."

The society explained in academic terms when word combinations like Soccer Mom should be considered a single entry for dictionary purposes:

"Many of the words chosen by members of the Society are in fact compounds consisting of two words or more. That is because new coinages are often formed by combin-

ing words. Such multi-word compounds are so frequent in English that they are found on nearly every page of a dictionary.

"Spelling lags behind, keeping the components separate even as they form a compound different from the sum of its parts.

"But pronunciation tells when a combination is a single dictionary entry rather than a casual phrase. A compound will have stress on the first words, as in 'SOCcer mom,' while a casual phrase will have stress on the last word, as in 'overworked MOM.' Only the former is eligible for consideration as a Word of the Year. The latter is merely two separate words."

Checking Out
the Sideline Types

A soccer sideline of parents offers plenty of people-watching opportunities in case you get bored with the game (such as when your kid is out for a rest). See if you can spot any of these types who sometimes are seen on the sidelines.

Moms

Clothes Horse

Moms who just raced to an early evening game from the office are excused for being overdressed for the occasion. No excuse for anyone who looks like she's attending a theatre benefit or riding to hounds.

Snob

The other parents aren't good enough for her socially, so she just ignores them. She doesn't deign to come to many games, and when she does, she only watches when her child is playing.

Paranoid

Someone is always out to get her player or team, most especially the referee. Paranoia level increases exponentially at road games ("They put us on the smaller field because we like to spread out;" "they wet down the field because we're fast."). Sometimes paranoids cancel each other out (True example from a league with teams in Maryland and Virginia: Maryland mom—"Those Virginia refs are out to get us every time." Virginia mom—"I hate to play in Maryland; their refs are out to get us every time.")

Screamer

Bring your ear plugs. Her high pitch adds to your agony. Different from the male yeller, who uses words. The screamer just shrieks. Close relative to the pounder, an indoor soccer phenomenon who beats in joy on the plexiglass window overlooking the playing surface.

Clueless

After years of watching kid soccer, she still has no idea what offside is, and doesn't care.

Cheerleader

Makes the team banner; provides special snacks unannounced; wears the team colors to every game.

Three Faces of Eve

She has a totally different view of any team issue each time she's asked.

Storekeeper

You need it, she's got it. Band-Aid? Ice? Scissors? Schedule?

Huntress

Most often an unmarried friend of a mom who sights fresh prey among the dads.

Chatterbox

Keep moving unless you want to hear every detail of her kids' activities ranging from classroom exams to doctor exams.

Foster Soccer Mom

Takes care of the kids on the team whose moms don't want to be, or can't be, real Soccer Moms.

Specialist

Her kid asks, "Who are we playing?" She replies, "I do the when, the where and the wash; you do the who, the what and the why."

Dads

Yeller

Comments at the top of his lungs throughout the game on everything, including the referee's ancestry, the outrageous fouls committed by the opponent, and what his son ought to be doing with the ball. Can sometimes be seen watching the game from the parking lot after banishment by the referee.

Reader

Today's newspaper is more interesting than the game. Usually will look up if Susie is his daughter and someone shouts, "Good play, Susie."

Isolationist

Watches the game intently, away from the bother of the other parents. Often a Type "A" personality.

Lech

Hits on any attractive and unattached female who shows up on the sideline. Warn your friends.

Expert

Offers an authoritative-sounding explanation for any confusing ruling or situation that arises on the field or in the conduct of the league or a tournament. Sometimes he's right.

Clocker

Wears a sports watch, actually remembers to start the timer at the kickoff, and always knows how much time is left in the half. Quick to criticize the officials for mistiming or for adding too much or too little injury time.

Scout

Goes to lots of other games in the age group. Can tell you the playing background and potential availability of every good player in the area.

Cameraman

Hauls portable scaffolding and suitcases of equipment to shoot material for a feature film-length video on his son that will be sent to 100 college coaches (and viewed by none.)

Closet Critic

Often criticizes the coach to other parents, especially as the coaching relates to his kid's playing time or position, but won't talk to the coach about his concerns.

Attacker

Nothing his kid does is right. He should have passed the ball sooner, or held it longer. She should have gone for the near post instead of the far post, or the far post instead of the near post. He should have taken that forward down instead of letting him get in close for a goal. He shouldn't have committed that foul.

Defender

Nothing his kid does is wrong. There was no need to pass off because she usually can handle four defenders. He wouldn't have been faked out so badly if the grass had been mowed down like it's supposed to be. He wouldn't have had to punch an opponent and get red-carded if the other guy hadn't shouldered the ball away from him.

Sideline Insight

If you're a single mom who's considering joining up longterm with a single Soccer Dad, the sideline offers an excellent opportunity for assessing the temperament of your intended.

Make arrangements to meet him at his kid's game. Arrive just after the game starts, then watch from a distance. What's his temperament? Does he encourage or disparage his child? Does he berate the officials?

After some observation, walk up smiling and apologize for being a bit late. Does his behavior change when you're around? How do the other parents seem to get on with him? Does he take victory or defeat in appropriate spirit?

P.S. Remember that a suitor may check you out the same way at your kid's game.

Soccer Mom Self Portrait - IV

"I'm absolutely stressed out and totally exhausted at times, fighting to balance everything. Seeing my kids' enjoyment on the soccer field makes it all worth it and gives me motivation."

--Kim Johnston, Ohio
quoted in *Dayton Daily News*

Red Cards!! Yellow Cards!! Thank You Cards??

Surviving Referees and their Assistants

If you think being a Soccer Mom is a thankless task, try being a soccer referee.

Baseball umpires, football officials and basketball referees are beloved compared to the worldwide standard for soccer's "man in the middle" and his two assistants on the sidelines.

In some countries, stadium playing fields are surrounded by moats to keep angry fans away from officials.

Even in the United States, the international soccer governing body insisted on erecting chain link fences around the fields at some venues during World Cup '94.

In some highly reputable youth leagues, the regulations routinely list the procedures for dealing with physical assaults on officials.

When even the world's most experienced officials catch flak for their calls at international championship games, there's no reason to expect that the decisions will be unanimously acclaimed at an under-12 game refereed by a deskbound office worker trying to pick up a few extra bucks on the weekend.

At rec league games for the youngest players, coaches or parents with minimal training may draw the officiating duty. But at those levels, the offside rule generally isn't enforced and the play isn't rough enough to be a problem.

Most youth games are handled by certified referees. Yes, believe it or not, the refs have to pass an officiating course and also must attend periodic recertification clinics. As (and if) they become more competent as assessed by formal evaluators, referees can win certification to higher and higher levels of play, right up to approval by FIFA (the international soccer governing body) to officiate international games. Most, of course, like the players, don't make it that far.

The referee is in complete charge of the game once it begins. Because soccer is an international game with attendant potential language barriers, the referee uses hand and arm signals and the assistants on the sideline use flags to signal their rulings. The referee also shows a yellow card or a red card to a player to signal a warning or expulsion respectively.

The soccer rule book is relatively short as compared to other team sports, and much is left to the discretion of the referee. Fans, of course, don't always think he's so discreet. Like basketball officials, soccer referees can vary greatly in the extent to which they "let 'em play" or, conversely, call fouls on even very minor contact.

Most referees are male, but some are women who are assigned to boys' games as well as girls' games.

Some signs of a good referee include:

- He is properly attired and equipped.
- He moves up and down the field with the play, as opposed to watching from midfield with little movement (a common failing of refs with big beer guts.)
- Her signals are prompt, crisp and authoritative, not slow or uncertain.
- He ignores the usual player mutterings and discontent as long as the language isn't foul or personal, as opposed to having rabbit ears seeking an excuse to card an unhappy player.
- He keeps an eye on the assistants for their signals, as opposed to ignoring them and missing their calls of blatant fouls that occurred out of his view.

- Whether calling the game tight or loose, she is consistent.

The principal tasks of the assistant referees (called linesmen until 1996) are to rule on balls out of bounds, to signal offside violations, and to catch serious fouls away from the ball that are outside the referee's field of vision.

Until the players are around age 12 or 13, volunteer parents or others often act as assistant referees at youth games. Their duties are generally confined by the referee to ruling on balls out of bounds along the sidelines and perhaps endlines, but not calling offside or fouls.

In some areas, youths as young as 11 or 12 take the officiating courses and act as assistant referees. Part of the purpose of having very young officials is to try to engage people who will stick with officiating as they become adults. Unfortunately, young assistants are sometimes very timid about signaling offside or fouls. That, in turn, unleashes the bully in some parents who try to intimidate the youngsters in ways they would not try with an adult.

The bottom line:

- You will be infuriated by some referee decisions. You will become certain that eye-to-brain coordination gets more sluggish with age. But if youth game officials were perfect, they'd be working pro and international matches, not your kid's game.

- You will sometimes believe that the ref cost your kid's team the game when he makes a bad foul call, or misses an offside, or even says from his bad angle that a shot didn't completely cross the goal line although your view from the corner showed the ball was a valid goal. But don't forget those whiffed shots, defensive lapses and goalie's brainlock that also cost your team the game.

- Parents yelling about a bad call distract their players into focusing on the past ruling rather than the ongoing play. Distracted players make mistakes that can be more damaging than the bad call.

- You will encounter referees who act out in their supreme authority on the field, perhaps as a release from the shackles that bind them in their jobs or home lives. You won't overwhelm one of these auto-crats with your yelling or your sarcasm, so just shut up and hope the parents from the other team anger him more than your parents do.

- Especially in larger metropolitan areas, you will have many officials of foreign origin who bring cultural differences and perhaps a different brand of soc-cer experi-ences to the field. Re-member that soccer is an international game and that players may as well start getting used to the different re-gional and national approaches.

- Most leagues and tournaments offer some official channel for a coach to submit written comments about the officials. It may seem like talking on a dead telephone, but the comments usually do get read by referee assignors and evaluators.

- At some point, your team will have a game canceled because no officials could be found. As youth soc-cer grows rapidly, finding enough officials is an in-creasing problem. How much abuse would you put up with for $20 or $30?

Some Soccer Moms Aren't

The whole soccer mom thing is "political consultant baloney. The moms who are at these games could be at the beach or in a bar or having their hair done. But they're not. They're here. They have values. They want their children to grow into leaders. But does that make these mothers some sort of political block? No, it makes them mothers who go to soccer games."
--Rina Ortega, Florida
quoted in *The Palm Beach Post*

"We don't deserve to be kicked around as a political football. Sometimes it comes off like we're all airheads, when actually we're politically astute and college educated with good incomes."
--Nancy Crane, Ohio
The Dayton Daily News

"I have a life other than being a soccer mom."
    --Diane McGowan, real estate agent, North Carolina
        quoted in [Wilmington, NC] *Morning Star*

"No. Absolutely no. Not at all. Don't mention me by that label. It sort of conveys this image of a woman driving around in her van, taking kids to soccer practice and spending all her time doing that, as if that's the sole point of her existence. It is just insulting."
    --Leslie Patterson, California
        quoted in *The Independent*

"Soccer moms? That's kind of insulting. Who are these soccer moms? What does that mean? Is that a euphemism for housewife? It seems sexist and old-fashioned. I don't go to all the games. Until I went to school I went to all the games. Sometimes [son Gage is] the only one there without a parent. I just tell him if he wants to play, he has to have the commitment himself."
    --Nancy Hills, teaching assistant and full-time master's degree candidate, California
        quoted in *San Francisco Examiner*

Soccer Mom Shoots on Goal

"The very first soccer mom, it is said, was Betty Broderick, a California housewife who came to fame in 1989 with four children, a four-wheel drive, and a license plate that read LODEMUP. But Betty didn't quite fit the type: far from tamely trawling her children to the Saturday game, she threw out her cheating husband, and later shot him dead with a .37."

The Independent

Soccer Mom Vacation Schedule

Like to travel? See new places? Make new friends?

Soccer Moms earn terrific vacations, including both weekend getaways and longer trips. The higher the level of your son's or daughter's competition, the more terrific vacations you'll get. Here's a sample year:

Labor Day Weekend

Drive four hours (including 90-minute rush hour penalty) on Friday afternoon/evening of Labor Day weekend to Labor Day Tournament site. Get up Saturday at 5:30 a.m. to feed player and get to field site 30 minutes from hotel in time for 7:30 a.m. warmups for 8 a.m. game. Keep players fed and entertained between games all weekend, with players always just short of enough time or enough energy to make it to the wonderful tourist attraction that enticed the team to the tournament city in the first place. Make it to the finals on Monday afternoon, so that your drive home is delayed until the height of the homebound holiday traffic.

Columbus Day Weekend

Drive five hours (including same rush hour penalty) to Columbus Day tournament at a beach city where the temperature has plunged to 44 degrees. Spend time between games at a mall with a food court and stores that are exactly the same as the ones at your hometown mall.

Weekend before Thanksgiving

Drive to the fall season's last outdoor tournament in a northern state. Enjoy the brisk 30-mile-per-hour winds, especially at the overtime final that concludes in the dark. Be thankful you have your auto club card when you become stuck in the mud at the 20-field complex laid out on a flood plain.

Week between Christmas and New Year's

Drive 15 hours to Florida for a four-day tournament. Be thankful that the snow you missed back home was only cold rain in Florida.

Mid-March Weekend

Attend local season-opening tournament only one hour (but six trips) away from home. Brisk winds doom your hairdresser's best work to look like you were practicing headers with it.

Memorial Day Weekend

Drive 10 hours to Cleveland for a two-day tournament. Game schedule doesn't leave enough time to go to the Rock 'n' Roll Hall of Fame.

Mid-July

Use all of your frequent flier miles to fly to a week-long tournament, and all of your frequent drug store points to purchase insect re-pellent.

Early August

Send your soccer player(s) to a sleepover soccer camp for a week and take a real vacation!

The Significance of "Soccer" in "Soccer Mom"

"'Soccer mom' is a phrase fraught with meaning, said Marshall Blonsky, a noted authority on semiotics -- the study of signs and systems of communication – who has made a career of probing the deeper cultural significance of our institutions and symbols. 'It's touching the live wire of contemporary ideology,' he said. The football mom was yesterday's mom, he said. Soccer, which is booming in popularity, rejects the 'symbolic killing' of rough-and-tumble football 'in favor of an aesthetic of flight, which makes it more modern than football.'"

The Washington Post

"The expression tells us that the female is watching sports now, and also, it tells us who she is watching. The irony of soccer is that while America is almost the only country in the world that has never made soccer numero uno, or even numero duo, tres or quatro, it is also the only country in the world where soccer is naturally perceived as androgynous. Indeed, our women gold medalists in Atlanta do better than our men. In no other country are there soccer moms watching soccer daughters play. . . The mere fact that the term 'soccer mom' has come into such accepted usage means, all the social implications aside, that soccer has moved up a step in our culture. Would it have meant anything to say 'badminton moms'? 'Water polo moms'?"

--Frank DeFord, commentator

National Public Radio, Morning Edition

Who Coined "Soccer Mom?"

No one knows who coined the colorful term, although it quickly gained popularity with the media and [political] strategists.

The Hartford Courant

Many analysts attribute the term to a man - a Seattle-based Republican political consultant named Brett Bader. Bader said he did coin the term "angry white male" to describe backers of the Republican landslide in 1994. But he wouldn't take the credit for the new label. "My wife's a soccer mom," he said. "But I didn't make it up."

The Denver Post

The term "soccer mom" to represent a voting bloc surfaced in mid August [1996], popularized, depending on who you believe (or your political persuasion) either by Republican consultant Alex Castellanos or Democratic consultant Dick Morris.

The [New Orleans] *Times-Picayune*

Susan B. Casey may well have coined the first political usage during Denver's 1995 municipal elections with her slogan "A Soccer Mom for City Council." It was, she thought, a way of denoting herself as everyneighbor.

The New York Times

How Much Is Enough?

Your player may be devoting too much time or attention to soccer if –

 The English teacher complains that he is using British English rather than American English spelling and expressions in his book reports.

 She turns down a date to the prom because it conflicts with the delayed tape telecast of a women's NCAA quarterfinal game.

 He can identify pentagons and hexagons in geometry class, but doesn't recognize a triangle or a rectangle.

 On a medical insurance registration card asking her age, she writes "U-13".

Asked in European history class to describe the Hanseatic League (of medieval German towns), he identifies it as the forerunner of the Bundesliga (the top German pro soccer league).

 Asked by a USA Today person-in-the-street reporter to comment on national defense policy, she states a preference for the sweeper/stopper setup rather than a flat back.

 Invited to a formal dinner party, he asks if that means he should wear his white uniform shirt with the collar rather than either the red collared shirt or the white-and-red T-shirt.

 Asked by a neighbor if she's been putting on weight, she says that yes, just last week she added 10 pounds to her bench press routine.

 When looking at wing-tip shoes to go with his job interview suit, he asks the clerk if they come in kangaroo leather.

The coach may be overdoing it if –

He requires players to watch game tapes that are longer than Bill Clinton speeches.

The five-mile pre-season conditioning run was one-way, with no transportation back.

He retains an agent to negotiate his contract with your son's team.

Her weekly phone report to you about your player lasts longer than the nightly newscast you were trying to watch.

The team got stuck overnight at Riverside Field when practice continued to its scheduled end despite the flood warning.

Soccer costs in your family may be getting out of hand if –

 Your daughter's favorite soccer store offers to open a branch outlet on your corner.

 Your family receives more soccer catalogs than magazines through the mail.

 The hospital emergency room that X-rayed your son's skull after that header collision, treated his twisted knee and removed his shattered toenail, is offering you its season ticket plan.

 You learn that the hotel's "special tournament rate" arranged by the tournament's exclusive booking agent is $7 a night higher than a family walking in off the street would pay.

 Your son has two pairs of $125 soccer shoes but no dress shoes.

You have to buy a new chest of drawers for your son to accommodate all the tournament T-shirts and sweatshirts he's bought.

 Your player is going to tournaments and soccer camps in more exotic locations, and more of them, than you've ever been able to afford for yourself.

 Your family has eaten soccer-ball-shaped pasta at dinner for 37 consecutive nights because you overcommitted to the team fund-raiser.

 Someone from the Imelda Marcos Museum called to inquire about your daughter's soccer shoes collection.

 You purchased $4,000 worth of computer equipment just so you could publish the team newsletter.

Soccer Mom Self Portrait - V

"After a dozen years on the sidelines in Ohio and Colorado, my findings suggest we may not be the simple, uniform demographic group that the cliches and generalizations would suggest. Soccer moms park 10-year-old Honda Accords  next to the Mercedes-Benzes, BMWs and 1974 Volkswagen Beetles  of other soccer moms. And we've carpooled to mansions and to apartment complexes where kids live in a third-floor walk-up. We're a lot more complicated than angry white males."

    --Diane Carman
        by-line article in *The Denver Post*

Doctor Mom

Doctor Mom of a youth soccer player should have most of the same attributes as the generic Doctor Mom of any child. But there are a few ailments and injuries associated with soccer that Doctor Mom might not otherwise see. Starting with the feet and working up--

The feet take a beating in soccer, not just from the running like in many other sports, but from the constant kicking of the ball and from being jabbed and stepped on in battles for the ball.

The nail of the big toe may sometimes blacken and either fall off or have to be removed if an infection settles in under the nail. Nail removal isn't as painful or traumatic as it sounds. Some players are back on the field within hours of a visit to the podiatrist.

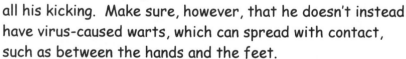

Your player may be proud of the calluses he thinks he's developing from all his kicking. Make sure, however, that he doesn't instead have virus-caused warts, which can spread with contact, such as between the hands and the feet.

Breaking in new soccer shoes can cause blisters and other pressure or friction problems with the feet. New shoes are supposed to fit tightly, in part for ball control and in part because the thin leather stretches easily. But even when shoes seem to fit properly, the hard uppers in the heel area can rub painfully, and the screw-in points of shoes with removable cleats can feel like blunt rods coming up through the bottom of the foot if the shoes are worn on hard ground better suited for shoes with molded cleats. Make sure your player has access to the various pads, shoe liners and heel cups that can reduce or eliminate discomfort.

Ankle twists and turns are as common in soccer as any other sport with quick stops and turns. The additional risk in soccer, however, is the kick in the ankle that sometimes is the result of a battle for the ball and sometimes is simply dirty play. Encourage your player to use shin guards that also have ankle protectors. Shin guards are mandatory for soccer, but ankle protectors are not. If your player has recovered from a recent ankle sprain or has a history of sprains, be sure he is taping his ankles for additional support or uses ankle braces. While a broken ankle, once healed, is usually as strong or stronger than it was before the break, the more sprains an ankle suffers, the more it will be susceptible to future sprains as the supporting structure becomes looser and looser. If your player apparently sprains an ankle, apply ice as quickly as possible to minimize swelling, then have it X-rayed to be certain whether the injury is a sprain, a break or a crack.

Leg and knee injuries in soccer usually are no different from those in any other running and contact sport. The instinct in soccer is to cart the player off to the side of the field as quickly as possible. But if a leg is obviously broken, insist on the player lying where she is until a medical crew can immobilize the leg before moving her.

Upper body and arm injuries are less frequent just by the nature of the sport. Rotator cuff and elbow problems are for baseball pitchers, not soccer players.

The head of a soccer player, however, is probably more vulnerable to concussion injuries than the heads of most other athletes simply because the head often is used to propel the ball. Some researchers recently have raised questions about whether repeated heading of the ball can lead to cumulative damage like that suffered by boxers from repeated punches. So far, the experts differ and the results of studies are inconclusive. The greater risk of injury is when two or more players go up simultaneously for an attempted header and whack heads instead of the ball. The forward or sideways thrust of the head used to add power to the header also adds power to the impact if it is accidentally against another head. Goal posts also can be a danger to heads. Players usually are aware of post location, but unstable temporary goals can surprise a player if they suddenly tip over. Most times, a player whose head is banged will suffer nothing more than a few moments of wooziness and perhaps an ugly bump. But always keep a close eye on the player for a time. Any loss of consciousness, sign of a memory failure, vomiting or sleepiness within the next couple of hours could mean a concussion serious enough that you should head for the emergency room right now.

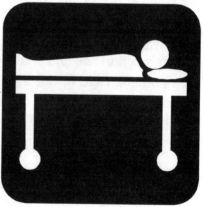

Mouth or tooth injuries also are an occasional product of heading gone awry. If your player wears dental braces, he should wear a mouthguard to reduce chances of mouth cuts from the metal or damage to the hardware.

In very warm weather, beware of heat stroke. Younger players often haven't yet learned to ration their energy during a game. Those who are active anyhow may tend to race around like madmen, making them especially vulnerable. Make sure your player is consuming plenty of fluids before the game and during every break. Keep an eye out for overly flushed skin, abnormally heavy breathing, difficulty swallowing, complaints of diarrhea, or staggering. In any such case, get the player out of the game, out of the sun, and cool him with water, cold cloths, or a ride in your air-conditioned car—and make that a ride to the emergency room if symptoms seem severe or prolonged.

Asthma is increasing in frequency among U.S. children. If your child is asthmatic, you're well aware of the danger signs. Make sure that the player always has an inhaler available, whether or not you're at the game or practice. Be especially vigilant when playing at unfamiliar fields, where the different combination of grasses and pollens may trigger an attack. Make sure the coach knows of your player's condition, and that your player knows to kneel or lie down on the field in the event of an attack so play will stop. He should not just wave a hand and wait for the next normal break in play.

Bee and insect stings and bites can be a product of playing on fields near woods and shrubs. Warn your player to check drink bottles and straws before taking a swig if the bottle has been near the ground attracting tiny visitors. A bee sting in the throat or red ant bite on the lips is no fun.

On the Road

Road trips to out-of-town soccer tournaments are a frequent event for the better select teams. The team Soccer Moms can have a definite impact on team performance at these tournaments through their control of players' meals, rest and off-the-field activities. Here are some guidelines to keep in mind.

 If the tournament is more than 60-90 minutes away, plan to stay at area lodging each night prior to a game day (usually Friday and Saturday nights). The team manager or other designated person should be booking rooms for the group. Make sure your player has at least a rollaway, if not a regular bed, to sleep on; sleeping on the floor can lead to stiffness that hampers play, especially on cold mornings.

Enforce whatever curfew the coach sets, or agree with the other parents on a bedtime that's appropriate both in light of age and wake-up time for the morning game.

Get up early enough in the morning for players to have a decent, non-greasy breakfast that can settle before they start playing. Calculate backwards from the kickoff time. For example:

8:00 a.m.	kickoff
7:15 a.m.	all players at field for warm-ups
6:45 a.m.	leave for field 25 minutes from hotel
6:00 a.m.	seated for breakfast
5:30 a.m.	wake up

Wake-up would be earlier if, for example, the hotel did not have breakfast service and you had to drive to a restaurant, the field was further away, directions or weather were uncertain, or the room was occupied by four or five people, increasing the line at the bathroom. Also remember that 15 or 20 people descending on a just-opening restaurant for breakfast can overwhelm the staff for a time, making service slow.

Make sure the team manager gives you adequate directions, preferably including a map. Don't just assume you can follow someone. This is even more important if you are staying with friends or relatives instead of at the team hotel.

Bring an adequate range of on-field clothing for all potential weather conditions, including early morning cold and heavy rain.

Bring enough water or sports drinks for potential conditions, including afternoon heat at a field with no shade trees.

At most tournaments, each team plays two games on the first day; the second game typically begins 2-4 hours after the first ends, although the break occasionally is as short as an hour. Unless the break is very short, the players normally will eat between games. Have them eat as soon after the first game as practical so the food has more time to settle. Pasta or deli sandwiches are better than hamburgers and fries. Food courts are good choices because there is a variety of food, self-service is quicker than table service, and there is no hassle over check-splitting and tip calculation.

Don't let your player use the swimming pool, ocean or lake between games. Water deadens the legs for a time; save the swimming for after the last game of the day.

Encourage activities that keep players off their feet for at least part of the time between games, especially in hot weather. A movie is much better than strolling the boardwalk or a mall.

 Save the more extensive sightseeing for after the second game or after the tournament. Unfamiliar drives, lines and other unexpected time-users just put unneeded stress on both parent and player if the deadline for being back on the field is getting close. Players also are usually tired for a time after the game, and likely won't appreciate the attraction anyway.

 Don't overprotect or isolate your player. A significant value of tournament trips is the opportunity for the players to get to know each other better and to bond, especially when they are from a number of different schools and neighborhoods. It's okay for your player to ride with some other team family for a few hours instead of joining you for a side trip to that wonderful museum of ancient Mayan art that you (but not she) has always wanted to visit. If you are staying with friends or relatives rather than at the team hotel, be especially alert to give the player significant time with team friends.

 If your player goes off with others, don't send him with an empty pocket. Each player and family should be prepared to foot their own expenses at tournaments.

Bring a small box of laundry detergent and a half a roll of quarters, because you'll probably have to find a laundromat at the hotel or nearby, at least for the uniforms, especially if it is rainy or the field is muddy. Remember before midnight to do this task or you will grow amazingly frustrated with a dryer that takes longer and digests more coins than you ever thought possible.

Be aware of what entertainment or programs the tournament is offering (dance, party, college soccer game, forum with college coaches, etc.) but recognize that the kids usually will reach peer consensus about what activities they want to go to and what they don't.

Don't drag a team of kids to fancy restaurants. You'll waste their interest and your money. At more casual table-service restaurants, let the players (about 12 or older) eat at their own tables, but tell the waiter to automatically add 15-20 per cent for the tip. Waiters are generally more accepting of team table antics if they know they won't be stiffed. Parents can then sit in a different part of the restaurant and enjoy adult conversation and fare.

If attending a three-day tournament (which are common over three-day holiday weekends), make sure you know what kind of check-out slack the hotel is allowing teams that get eliminated on the second day and so don't have to stay that night. Sometimes you may have to check out and then check back in again if your team unexpectedly advances to the third day.

Don't set up incentives to lose by promising glamorous side trips for Sunday afternoon if the team is eliminated Sunday morning (Hey, play hard, but if you guys don't make the finals, we can stop for a few hours at Wonder-World on the way home!)

Don't expect a paid coach to baby-sit or entertain players at any point unless he expressly offers, for example, to take them to a college or pro game.

Finally, don't assume you have to go to every tournament if you find it's a drag or just doesn't fit your schedule of work or care for your other kids. Ask another family well in advance if your player can ride and stay with them. Sometimes that allows two older kids to have an even better time by sharing a separate room. Just remember to send enough money with your player to cover meals, entertainment, the appropriate share of the room, and an offer to help with the gasoline. Conversely, be prepared to help someone with a ride and room at another tournament.

Dealing with Macho

Soccer brings out men's worst macho instincts. Consider:

- The testosteronic grunts and shoulder twitches of the fellows at the next table of a sports bar that caters to soccer fans. Double the meter reading if they're from a European or Latin-American soccer country.

- The co-worker whose autocratic "I can do no wrong" behavior puzzles you in light of his mid-level job position and performance—until you learn that he referees half a dozen soccer games every

weekend.

- The dads who knew nothing about soccer until their kids got involved, but now assume they know far more than you know about the game despite your spending as many or more years on the sideline.

- The coach who always phones or seeks out the dad, not the mom, for player appraisal conversations, especially if the player is a boy.

- Your son, the player, who, especially if he's into the teen years, will totally tune you out if you try to offer any constructive suggestions about his skills or tactics.

Coping with macho begins early. As your young child's team swarms around the little size 3 ball like bumble bees, it will be the moms' station in life to provide the juice, the transportation to practice, and the encouragement. Fathers appear at the games on Saturdays or Sundays to talk with other fathers about pro sports, compare their offspring's prowess with the other children's, and offer expert (but often wrong) comment about the game. Dads get to do the "real soccer" tasks like lining the field, setting up the nets, fielding errant pre-game practice kicks, and most prestigious of all, serving as a volunteer linesman to assist the sole official. Moms get to bring the quartered oranges, half-time drinks and post-game treats, and bandage the skinned knees and elbows.

As the years roll on with a boys' team, the macho flows from the fathers to the sons as naturally as the Mississippi. And the dads take the credit for it all. If the team is fairly stable, the boys have bonded tighter than glue. They now ignore Mom's soccer observations as a unit, rather than individually. Mom can't run onto the field anymore when there's a skull clash. (Mom: unless an ambulance is called, stay off the field). One saving grace is that the coach is no longer calling and asking if your husband is available. He's not calling at all, because by this age, the players are getting their appraisals directly—sometimes in words of one syllable that wouldn't please Miss Manners.

Your family used to save money at the tournament hotel by all staying together in a single room, sometimes with a player or two sleeping on the floor. Now the players want to share their own rooms separate from Mom—and Dad. Your major hotel role is as the relay station for calls from the desk clerk passing on complaints from other guests about the noise from the room your player is sharing with a teammate or two. Your best move is cheerfully to say "Sure!" when your player asks if he can ride with another parent to the field or restaurant or mall. These guys move everywhere in macho herds. If it weren't for the numbers on their backs, it would be difficult to tell them apart.

Short of forcing your son to employ his speed, grace and coordination on the ballet stage instead of the soccer field, is there anything much to do about macho? You won't be able to curb its inherent existence. But if you want to at least be listened to, and have some influence on your player's team, it's not that difficult except, perhaps, in the most old-world of soccer cultures. Like most other activities from community politics to charitable fund-raising, the main ingredients for respect and influence are learning the subject and taking on some tasks. Careful observation can provide much of the learning. Remember, if you just know the offside rule, you're ahead of many on the sideline. Ironically, the macho types often are flattered to be asked to explain some rule or strategy. The trick is having a sense of whether your "expert" knows what he's talking about. For a discussion of useful soccer tasks you might consider, see "If You Want a Job Done Right . . .", p. 141.

If you're not looking for influence or involvement, but just want to keep up with how your player is doing, try to establish a once or twice per season dialogue with the coach. Focus on what your player can do to improve, and get the coach to evaluate your player in comparison with other players in understandable terms. If you seek explanations rather than confrontations, you'll probably get a more useful response. If the first response is too general or too evasive or too technical, just keep asking "why?" or "could you explain that some more." If a paid coach is giving you a macho runaround, remind him who's paying his fee.

Of course other ways to deal with macho are to just confront it briefly and then walk away, or to walk away in the first place. If the coach is too imperious or condescending, don't hesitate to give him a brief piece of your mind. Coaches don't cut players because of their parents except in the most obnoxious or destructive situations.

When the macho gets too deep for your boots, always remember that the sideline is 100 or more yards long. If that doesn't get you far enough away from the protagonists, well, at a lot of fields you can park close enough to get a pretty decent view of the game from your car. And don't forget your copy of *Vanity Fair* for the halftime break (or in case the referee bans you to the parking lot due to your expert appraisal of his calls).

Wow! My Kid Really IS a Good Player!

There is always opportunity for a good soccer player to improve and to play at a higher level of competition.

For many good players, the major step up will be from recreation to select as 9-to-11 year-olds. For the best players at each level, however, another higher level will beckon.

Soccer Mom (and Dad) have the rewarding task of encouraging and facilitating the climb as far as the player has the desire, ability and determination to go. But they must not make the mistake of pushing a player beyond the player's interest or capabilities.

The space in the soccer pyramid, like any other pyramid, gets a lot smaller as the top nears. But thanks to Title IX for women and the recent development of Major League Soccer for men, there are new high-level soccer opportunities that create a positive impact down through the pyramid.

If you're assuming a full ride through college on an athletic scholarship or a spot on a national team for your young soccer player, however, get a grip on numerical reality quickly!

For example:

■ About 300,000 boys are playing high school soccer this year.

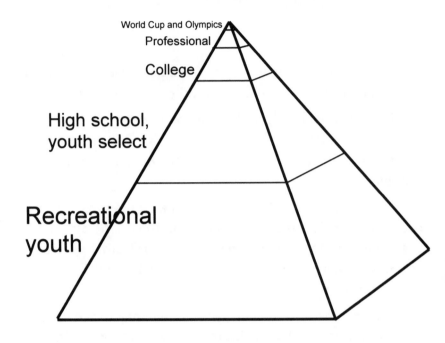

World Cup and Olympics
Professional
College
High school, youth select
Recreational youth

The U.S. Soccer Pyramid

Volumes of players in selected categories

■ About 700 members of the National Collegiate Athletic Association (NCAA) have men's soccer teams. That's roughly 15,000 roster spots, or one for every 20 boys who played high school soccer. Numerous smaller colleges in the National Association of Intercollegiate Athletics (NAIA) and many two-year community colleges also field teams.

■ Nearly 400 four-year colleges (both NCAA and non-NCAA) offer some form of soccer scholarships to men, ranging from full tuition, room and board, to a bit of help with tuition. The number for women is about the same. Each NCAA school is limited to a maximum of 9.9 full scholarships for men and 12 for women, and many choose not to offer that many. For the NCAA members, that's less than one scholarship for every five roster spots, or less than one for every 100 boys who played high school soccer.

Or how about a spot on a national youth team?

■ Each state has an Olympic Development Program (ODP). About 25 players in each age group, starting usually at U-13, are selected for the state ODP team (two teams in a few populous states).

■ From these state teams, about 25 players are picked for each of four regional teams, and then from the regional teams, a national pool of 25-40 players is selected.

■ From these national pools, teams of about 18 are picked for international youth competition at several age levels starting with U-15. That's 18 out of perhaps 75,000 to 100,000 players in the age group for boys, and of perhaps 50,000 to 70,000 girls.

Envisioning a trip to the Olympics or World Cup to watch your player?

- 🏴 For men, the Olympics is an under-23 tournament. Olympic coaches usually select professional and college players after a series of camps and games that goes on for many months in advance of the Olympics.

- 🏴 For women, the Olympics are open to players of any age, the same as for the quadrennial Women's World Cup. Some players are fresh from college while others are under professional contract to the national team and perhaps also playing abroad.

The World Cup is soccer's most prestigious event. Members of the U.S. national team almost always have at least several years of professional experience in overseas leagues and/or, since 1996, Major League Soccer. Team qualifying for the World Cup goes on over about a two-year period. The national team also plays in other international competitions, and is an ever-changing cast. For each competition, the coach calls up the particular players he wants, sometimes taking newer players to give them experience and evaluate them for future competition.

Well, maybe your kid won't ever be in the World Cup, but after several years of play, it's obvious he or she is darned good.

It's not just you, or only the other parents on the team, or even just your coach who says so. You hear about compliments from other coaches. She is approached about joining better teams. You can sense his growing confidence and presence.

What do you do, notwithstanding some of the numbers cited above?

Two things: provide support and present opportunities.

Support

Support can take many forms:

- Verbal encouragement of the immediate play or game, but especially of the player's longer-term soccer plans and aspirations. Don't tell her she can't achieve her goal even if it sounds impossibly high to you. Instead, counsel her on how to map out a step-by-step plan to get to the goal, and then help her concentrate on achieving the next step.
- Logistical help so the player gets to practices and games on time.
- Finances to pay for team dues, shoes, uniforms, out-of-town travel and the other costs of soccer,

or, if the budget is tight, help for the player to plan how he'll earn the money or get the outside assistance.

 Providing proper nutrition and rest.

 Your own attendance at games.

 Taking on your share, or more, of the adult tasks that are necessary, or at least desirable, for the functioning of the team.

This kind of support is nice, of course, for a player at any level. But the better the player, the more important it becomes because the demands on the player are greater, and the costs in time and money for the player and family increase substantially.

Opportunities

Players, especially as they get older, may know about opportunities from coaches, friends and their own reading before you do. But as your player demonstrates a desire to play at a higher level, you should begin doing your own information gathering so he'll know what is available.

Remember, however, that your role is to present the opportunities to the player for her consideration and decision. The younger the player, the more you'll be able to influence the decision. But don't turn off a player mentally about some soccer activity because "you made me go."

Some of the school-age opportunities for interested and qualified players were mentioned in the earlier section, "Is My Kid Any Good at Soccer?" Here is more information on those and other more advanced opportunities:

Select Teams

Some rec leagues are part of organizations that have their own select teams. Other select teams are affiliated with soccer clubs that do not have recreation-level compe-

 tition. Parents of slightly older players are probably your best source of information. Also check the bulletin boards at soccer stores or the sports pages of small community newspapers for announcements of tryouts, which most often occur from June through August, and in March. The state youth soccer association also can provide names of leagues and clubs in your area.

In populous areas, there may be a broad range of opportunities. If your player is at the entry level age and teams are just forming, seek out the clubs or coaches with the best reputations for teaching and stability. Dad and Mom coaches are fairly common at the younger years of select play. Their experience varies greatly. Beware of the parent coach who is mostly looking for a cast of supporting players to surround his son, the star.

If your player is trying to join a team in an age group that has been competing for a season or more, try first with the most successful teams. If your player isn't selected, ask the coach for references to other teams he thinks are suitable.

Some players will stick with one select team through ten years of youth competition. Others, sometimes because of a parent who fancies himself as a sports agent, continually switch teams looking for some magical situation. Of course it's appropriate to look for another team if things aren't working out at the first stop, or if the player's ability and team's ability are a mismatch. But if every stop is unhappy, consider that the fault may be that of the player or parents, not that of a succession of coaches and teams.

Small-Sided Tournaments

In addition to the tournaments your team enters, look for small-sided tournaments, usually featuring 4-on-4 games for a half-day or day. They're both fun and good experience in a low-key setting, and it's usually easy to find three or four teammates who are available to play.

Guest Player

Most tournaments permit teams to bring along several guest players. Being a guest player offers a good opportunity to get some additional competition if your team is idle that weekend, or even to try out with another team. Looking for guest slots is a matter of talking to other teams in your area about their tournament plans and needs. Your coach may be able to help out, too.

Schools

It should go without saying that a strong player will try out for his school's team. Where the player has a choice of schools, either through a public school open enrollment plan or by selecting a private school, there may be an opportunity to upgrade his soccer experience by attending a school with a strong coach and program. Of course academics, cost and location are primary factors in school selection, but for the serious player entering high school, it's important to assess the soccer prospects, too.

Summer Camps

Soccer camps are a burgeoning business. Some are good. Others are glorified day care. Some camps meet for a half-day or full day near your home. Others are sleep-over camps, usually for one week, occasionally for two. Check with other players, parents and coaches for recommendations.

Don't assume that because a big-name coach is running the camp, he'll be tutoring your player; that task is carried out by the assistants, whose experience may vary greatly. Are they assistant college coaches or high school coaches, or are they only slightly older players doing their first instructing? What is the ratio of instructors to players?

There should be at least one for every team's worth of players (11-15). If your player is a goalie, be sure that a goalie coach will be on hand.

Check the age range of players attending the camp. Better players, especially as they hit the teen years, should be looking for chances to play with older players.

What is the typical daily schedule? Beware of too much time scheduled for the swimming pool or the gym. Also beware of combination camps such as a half-day of soccer and half-day of computers. There may be nothing wrong with the soccer training, but it is probably more suited for average or beginning players; strong players go to more intensive all-soccer camps. Similarly, half-day sessions are okay for young players, but a player 11 or older looking for significant training should go to an all-day or sleepover camp.

Overseas Soccer Trips

Some select or school teams take overseas trips to tournaments, or to play a series of friendly games. Other opportunities to play abroad are offered by various organizations that put together teams for the specific purpose of a trip.

Whether a team or family wants to spend the serious money associated with overseas travel is a decision that should weigh not only the soccer but also the cultural and maturation opportunities of the trip. If the decision is to go, the risks and "buyer beware" principle inherent in any purchase of travel are all still present. In addition, know what you're getting in the way of actual soccer. Who are the opponents? What is the event? You may be guaranteed five games at a tournament—but are they full games or half-games? What kind of fields? Will you have practice facilities available? Are you certain about the age categories? If considering going with a made-up team, who are the coaches and the other players, and what are their skill and experience levels?

Overseas Soccer Camps and Training Programs

Deciding whether to send your
player to an overseas camp or training program combines the considera-
tions of camps and overseas trips
discussed above, plus a more rigorous
evaluation of whether the player is
really good enough to make the experience and expense worthwhile. The
world famous Tahuichi program in
Bolivia, for example, offers one-
month and one-year programs that
likely would overwhelm the less-than-exceptional player.

Olympic Development Programs (ODP)

ODP programs vary somewhat from state to state in
their timing and method of player selection. In general,
however, tryouts are held by age group to identify top players. Those selected participate in additional training that
leads toward selection of a state team to compete in one of
four regions of the United States against other state
teams. Based on these competitions, a regional team at
each age is selected to compete against other regions. In
turn, national pools at each age are selected. From those
pools, U.S. national teams are picked for international competition.

Contact your state youth soccer association for information on when and where ODP tryouts are held. The
methods of selecting and training ODP players are sometimes controversial and may seem to be highly arbitrary,
but "ODP" on a player's resume is a strong credential that
is nationally recognized, especially by college recruiters.

College

The pyramid of youth soccer players is narrowing drastically by the time it reaches the level of potential college players, and even more as it climbs to the group of high school players being recruited for college scholarships to play soccer. If by the junior year of high school, your player realistically wants to compete in college, then it's time to gather information and take action. Here are a few key points:

Know the rules and requirements. The academic requirements for high school grades and SAT or other entrance exam results govern whether your player can compete as a freshman. The recruiting rules govern contacts between player and school. They are incredibly complex. For example, your player can telephone a college coach and ask for informa- 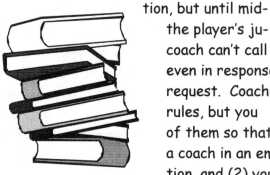 tion, but until midsummer after the player's junior year, the coach can't call the player, not even in response to a voice mail request. Coaches should know the rules, but you want to be aware of them so that (1) you don't put a coach in an embarrassing position, and (2) you can guard against an overzealous coach endangering your player's future eligibility.

Begin gathering information and making inquiries to schools during the junior year. Don't expect personalized responses, but do respond promptly to requests for information from schools in which the player continues to have an interest.

Make sure your player speaks or writes for himself or herself in all contacts with prospective schools. You may think you're a better letter writer or more articulate on the phone. But the coach wants a player, not a parent, and it is the player, not the parent, who will be attending the school. A well-composed soccer resume is appropriate, and some coaches will look at a 10-minute video if it is properly made. But a parent who peppers the coach with over-hyped "news" about the player is a definite turn-off.

Seek playing time exposure to coaches. Some major tournaments for U-17 to U-19 teams are magnets for coaches. Make sure your player's team is entering as many of them as feasible. If the player is interested in a school close to home, let the coach know the team schedule and solicit observation.

After gathering information, focus on a half-dozen or so schools. Be realistic about whether the player is a regional ODP and Parade All-American that the nation's top coaches will fight over, or is an all-county honorable mention whose best soccer bet is at a Division III school. Also be realistic academically. Don't expect a C student to play for Stanford or Duke just because he scores a lot of goals.

Choose a school, not just a soccer coach or program. Do the academics and course offerings match the player's future aspirations? Is the location geographically and socially agreeable? A good question for the player to ask is: "If I sustained a soccer career-ending injury after my first season, would I still want to attend this school?"

Professional Teams

Beyond college, or occasionally in place of college, lies the lure of a professional contract. The advent of Major League Soccer has created about 200 new top-level player opportunities in the United States (about 50 of them slotted for foreign players). Minor league opportunities in the A-League and USISL also have strengthened, and indoor play continues in pro leagues. A handful of U.S. players also get contracts to play overseas in leagues ranging from the best in the world to the deep minors. Women's professional playing opportunities to date are only with the U.S. national team and a few foreign leagues. But plans are afoot to start a U.S. women's league by 1999.

A significant point of controversy in men's play is whether college competition is of much help to the relatively few outstanding players who can realistically look toward pro careers. The college season lasts less than four months, but players cannot compete for clubs during the remainder of the academic year. U.S. college players simply play a lot less soccer during the 18-22 age span, and against generally weaker competition, than do European and South American players, who mostly are apprenticing or playing with club teams. Major League Soccer's Project 40 signs about 40 U.S. high school graduates each year to professional contracts (mostly to play in the minors at first). In lieu of the college athletic scholarships that some are giving up, Project 40 provides players with earmarked funds for an eventual college education as part of the deal. A very few U.S. high schoolers also go to Europe to apprentice with clubs.

Soccer Mom Self Portrait - VI

"In my mind, a soccer mom is someone really into the game. I'm probably too much of a soccer mom. Right now, it's my life."
--Kelly Burnett, California
quoted in *Fresno Bee*

"Soccer Mom" Label —

"Stop calling her Soccer Mom. No political analyst would refer to a father who worked, did 18 things around the house and coached Jimmy's football league on Saturday mornings as a Football Pop."

> --Froma Harrop,
> Rhode Island
> *Providence Journal-Bulletin*

"I find it condescending, the idea of identifying these women by what they do for their children."

> --June S. Speakman,
> political science
> professor, Rhode
> Island
> *The Hartford Courant*

"I don't like that phrase 'soccer moms.' It's condescending and it gives a very misleading concept of the lives most suburban women lead. I don't know of many women whose lives are centered around just driving their kids from one activity to another. Because of economic pressures, most of them have to work outside of the home. Their lives are hectic, always trying to catch up. That's a big part of the problems we've got ourselves into in this country. I know because I'm the older version of the soccer mom."

> --Ronna Romney, former U.S. Senate candidate,
> Michigan
> *The Detroit News*

Soccer in Print

There are plenty of sources for soccer families to pursue for news and information in print about the sport, but their accessibility and timeliness vary greatly.

In general, timely news about professional and top-level national teams is relatively easy to locate in daily newspapers of major soccer areas like Los Angeles, New York, Boston and Washington D.C. It gets tougher as locations become more distant from the cities that have (1) a Major League Soccer team; (2) a tradition of strong minor league professional soccer; (3) a history of hosting national team games; or (4) a very strong college team.

Soccer America is the most reliable weekly source of information about international, national and U.S. college soccer. *Soccer America* also includes biweekly features on youth soccer and a comprehensive monthly calendar of upcoming youth tournaments. It also publishes as part of its regular sequence annual directories of soccer camps, college soccer programs, and soccer shoes. *Soccer America* does not carry youth results, however, except at the national youth team and national club championship levels.

Soccer Jr. is a monthly magazine aimed at kids 12 or younger. It focuses on features, how-to, and personalities. Most state youth soccer associations publish newspapers or newsletters two to four times a year. These typically have a mix of how-to articles, discussions of youth soccer topics, and results that normally are quite dated, though useful for reference purposes.

Regional magazines or newsletters are beginning to appear in some soccer hot-beds. In the Maryland-Virginia-Washington D.C. area, for example, *Washington Soccer Net* publishes weekly pages of current youth league and tournament results, plus articles on area professional, college, adult amateur and high school competition. *Southern Soccer Scene* focuses on the South.

The Instep, published quarterly, offers information on college soccer scholarships. *Performance Conditioning for Soccer* offers excellent workout and conditioning guidance for the advanced player.

Some leagues or large clubs also circulate newsletters, sometimes to all participants and sometimes to their leadership. Soccer equipment and apparel companies, as well as some major national sponsors of soccer, offer a variety of catalogs and pamphlets that include useful information.

Soccer stores and mail order houses stock a vast array of training books and videos for coaches and older players.

A parent who is asked to manage a youth soccer team should pick up a copy of *What? ME Manage the Soccer Team?* It's full of information that makes handling team logistics easier. An order form is at the back of this book.

Soccer America (weekly)
(subscriptions and orders)
P.O. Box 16718
North Hollywood, CA 91615-6718
818-760-1562

Soccer Jr. (monthly)
27 Unquowa Rd.
Fairfield, CT 06430
203-259-5766

Soccer magazine (bimonthly)
5211 S. Washington Avenue
Titusville, FL 32780
407-268-5010

The Instep (quarterly)
Suite 6-1333
5030 Champion Blvd.
Boca Raton, FL 33496
561-995-6587

Performance Conditioning for Soccer (9/yr)
PO Box 6819
Lincoln, NE 68506
800-578-4636

Reedswain Inc. (soccer videos and books)
612 Pughtown Road
Spring City, PA 19475-3310
1-800-331-5191

Soccer on the Internet

Soccer news and information is big on the Internet. If any in your family are becoming fans of soccer at the international level, the internet will be your fastest source of scores from all over the world, including matches involving national teams and league play from all the major soccer countries.

The easiest way to track down soccer information is to tap into *Soccer America's* web site at

http://www.socceramerica.com

Soccer America is the principal national soccer publication, appearing weekly. Its web site is a joint effort with the Soccer Industry Council of America. It provides links to all kinds of professional soccer news and booster group sites, as well as information on college soccer. Scores, schedules, and TV listings for major games are staples at this site.

If you want a feel for the international governance of soccer, try logging into

http://www.FIFA.com

This is the Zurich-based site for the Federation Internationale de Football Association (FIFA).

Information on youth soccer is scattered. The U.S. Youth Soccer Association, some state associations, and various leagues, tournaments, clubs and even individual teams maintain web sites of widely varying quality and completeness, most of which can be located by starting at *Soccer America's* site.

One site that appeals to younger players is at

http://www.soccerpatch.com

Numerous colorful club patches are displayed there. Teams traveling to tournaments traditionally trade patches after each game with their opponents, so after a time, players accumulate scores of these embroidered souvenirs.

Search engines also can turn up soccer information. Run a search on "Soccer Mom" and you may find such personalized information as the biography at an IBM web site of a company program director in northern California who "is a veteran soccer mom, spending her time on the sidelines watching her kids play about 100 games a year."

Or, you might come across the personal web page of an upstate New York woman who comments how sometimes "I become glued to our van driver's seat because of all the chauffeuring I do. (I'm a hockey MOM, soccer MOM, track MOM, college-kids MOM, and now I am a MOM-IN-LAW!)"

Soccer Excuses
for Globe Trotting

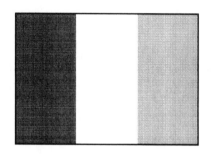

France

Summer 1998

World Cup '98

Quadrennial world championship
Men's national teams
June 10 - July 12, 1998

Bordeaux	Marseilles	Paris
Lens	Montpellier	St. Etienne
Lyon	Nantes	Toulouse

New Zealand

Winter 1999

Under-17 Boys Championship

Bienniel world championship
Boys' under-17 national teams
February - March, 1999

134

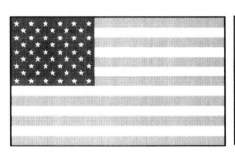

United States

June 1999

Women's World Cup

Quadrennial world championship
Women's national teams

Nigeria

Summer 1999

World Youth Championships

Bienniel championship
Men's under-20 national teams

Australia

Summer-Fall 2000

Olympic Games

Men's national under-23 teams
Women's national teams
September 15 - October 1, 2000

Sydney

Adelaide
Brisbane

Canberra
Melbourne

Argentina
2001

World Youth Championships

Bienniel championship
Men's under-20 national teams

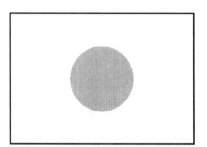

Korea   and   Japan

Summer 2002

World Cup 2002

Quadrennial world championship
Men's national teams

Soccer Mom Self Portrait - VII

"I guess we all volunteer and are average, middle class folks. We're just the same as everybody else. Unlike earlier generations, moms today are making the decisions and not playing second fiddle to anybody. And our kids are our lives."

    --Toni DuGal, Idaho
        quoted in *The Idaho Statesman*

If You Want a Job Done Right...

For every youth soccer team, there is another team—this one comprised of adults—doing the often unseen tasks that get the kids on the field. For the Soccer Mom who wants, or is at least willing, to do more than just ferry her player back and forth to practices and games, there are many opportunities to pitch in.

It's a good thing that past experience with soccer is no requirement, because the vast majority of today's Soccer  Moms didn't start learning about the sport until their player got involved. Even coaching at the entry-age levels is open to inexperienced moms who are willing to take the basic coaching clinic that many recreation leagues usually must offer in order to get enough coaches. Six-year-olds aren't concerned with offsides, tactics or even much in the way of skills, so their first coach doesn't have to be the master of advanced techniques. In fact, a mom's ability to organize kids and keep everyone moving and active is a bigger asset at this age than knowing four ways to put a curve on a kick. (Before long, the skyrocketing number of girls who started playing in the 80's will start becoming Soccer Moms themselves, and will be obvious candidates for coaching jobs now dominantly held at all levels by men.)

At the youngest ages, the coach usually also handles the few administrative tasks, perhaps with a mom in charge of the drinks and snacks. As teams get older and more competitive, someone other than the coach, often a mom, usually becomes team manager. This is mostly a communications and logistics job that begins with basic registration paperwork and can evolve to tasks such as producing a newsletter, preparing a budget, purchasing uniforms and equipment, making hotel and travel arrangements, and coordinating the hiring of a paid coach. Generally, the more advanced and older the team, the more man-agement is required. The manager often may ask other parents to volunteer for particular jobs. For ex-

ample, if you're a journalist, you're a natural to edit the newsletter. If you're in real estate, you ought to be preparing the maps and directions for finding the sites of road games. (If you volunteer or are drafted to become team manager, get a copy of *What? ME Manage the Soccer Team?*, a handbook of information, checklists and examples for team managers and coach/managers. See the last pages of this book for more information.)

In addition to the team jobs of coach, manager, or assistant coach or manager, an interested Soccer Mom can volunteer at the club or league level. Many clubs, for example, put on tournaments, and need people for jobs like producing a program, coordinating the competition in an age group, locating concessionaires, buying trophies, securing field permits and even arranging for portable toilets.

Fund-raising offers plenty of opportunities at both the team and club levels. The team may need leadership for a car wash or candy sale that is raising money for uniforms or a trip. The club may need volunteers to solicit corporate sponsorships or program advertisements to finance a tournament. The club or a group of clubs may even be raising serious money to build a new field complex. Your professional experience or contacts may make you a very valuable component of the fund-raising effort.

A mom looking for the combination of a fitness oppor-

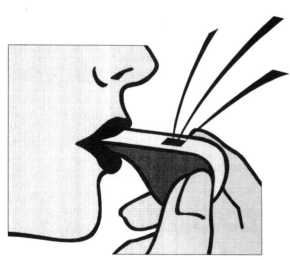

tunity and some extra money should consider getting a referee license. Working several hours of games on Saturday or Sunday as a referee or assistant referee could be worth as much as $100. Refs also get to wear fuchsia shirts (the color of the cover of this book). Check with your league or state association for information about required courses. An initial course qualifying you to handle younger games typically meets for about four evenings. In most areas, assignments are handled by a referees association under agreement with leagues and tournaments. An annual recertification course is required, plus additional training if you aspire to officiate at higher levels.

Moms who get into coaching can take courses to qualify for six levels of licenses recognized nationally. Some leagues and clubs require coaches of select or older teams to be licensed. Leagues or state associations have information on coaching courses.

The Soccer Mom Dictionary

Term	Definition Before Becoming a Soccer Mom	Definition After Becoming a Soccer Mom
area	portion of a building or land having a specific function, such as dining area or play area	18-by-44-yard area in front of each goal in which goalie can touch the ball with hands, and in which a foul by a defender may result in a penalty shot; includes the box (see "box"); formally called the penalty-area
ball	formal dance party, often held as a charity fund-raiser	most important piece of soccer equipment, usually found on kitchen floor or stairs
banana	yellow Central American fruit	kind of kick in which the soccer ball curves
bicycle	two-wheeled, self-propelled mode of transportation, usually not popular with children as a means of getting to sports practice if a car and driver are available	kind of kick in which the kicker rolls onto his hands, arms or shoulders, back of head to the goal, and kicks the ball with his legs in the air

Term	Definition Before Becoming a Soccer Mom	Definition After Becoming a Soccer Mom
boots	footwear for hiking or use in snow	soccer shoes
box	container for shipping goods	6-by-20-yard area in front of each goal in which goalie has extra protection from contact by offensive players; formally called the goal-area
chip	flat, crisp snack food made from potatoes or corn, consumed in large quantities by children and teenagers	shot on goal or pass gently kicked over the head of a close or onrushing opponent
counter-attack	furious cleaning of the kitchen when in-laws unexpectedly call to say they'll arrive in an hour	offensive attack quickly mounted after interrupting opponents' attack; intended to catch opponents' defenders out of position
cup	cooking measure; 8 ounces	name for many levels of soccer championships, e.g., World Cup, MLS Cup, State Cup, etc.

Term	Definition Before Becoming a Soccer Mom	Definition After Becoming a Soccer Mom
direct	instruct the performers in a stage show or motion picture	following certain fouls, a kick which is permitted to score a goal without being touched by any player other than the kicker
dribble	what a one-year-old does with her cereal; also, bounce a basketball	move with the soccer ball under close control by the feet

Term	Definition Before Becoming a Soccer Mom	Definition After Becoming a Soccer Mom
football	American game in which mostly oversized boys or men knock each other to the ground	name by which soccer is known everywhere else in the world except the United States
friendly	what you usually hope to be with your neighbors	a non-league, non-tournament game played under regular game conditions
fuchsia	shrubby plants of the prim-rose family	color of shirt often worn by officials
hand-ball	game played on an indoor court with a small rubber ball	illegal touching of a soccer ball in play with the hand or lower arm

147

Term	Definition Before Becoming a Soccer Mom	Definition After Becoming a Soccer Mom
header	identifying label at top of column or page of data or text	tactic of moving the soccer ball by striking it with the forehead
injury time	when, for example, your child breaks an arm falling off a bicycle	extra playing time added to each half of a soccer game to make up for time lost attending to injured players, or for other abnormal stoppages of play
keeper	a fish that, when caught, is large enough not to have to throw back into the water	shorthand term for the goal-keeper, especially used by the goalkeeper when yelling "KEEPER!" to teammates, indicating that he will catch or pick up an incoming ball; analagous to "I got it" in baseball

Term	Definition Before Becoming a Soccer Mom	Definition After Becoming a Soccer Mom
kick	what Frank Sinatra got from champagne	(*verb*) what players do with a soccer ball
		(*noun*) any of several plays that restart the game after a foul (direct kick, indirect kick) or after the ball goes over the endline (corner kick, goal kick).
kickoff	first play in American football	first play in real football
left back	what a child is when not promoted to the next grade in school	defensive player to the left of the sweeper
man on	warning cry familiar to moms who lived in college dorms before the dorms turned co-ed; for example, "Man on 2!"	warning yell to a teammate with the ball that a defender is approaching from behind or from the blind side; used by both boys and girls

Term	Definition Before Becoming a Soccer Mom	Definition After Becoming a Soccer Mom
match	small stick with chemicals on one end that catches fire and is used to set something else on fire	a soccer game
mid-field	terminal at Washington D.C.'s Dulles Airport that you must reach by taking a shuttle	center area of the soccer pitch
net	profits of a business after deducting expenses from revenues	what the ball is shot into for a goal
nutmeg	spice used in pumpkin pie	embarrass defender by kicking ball between defender's legs and regaining control, completing pass or scoring goal
own goal	major personal objective in life	accidentally deflect ball into your team's goal, thus giving opponents a score
Penta-gon	U.S. military headquarters in Washington, D.C.	shape of some of the panels on most soccer balls
pitch	salesman's spiel; also, the throwing of a ball toward the batter in the American game of baseball	soccer field

Term	Definition Before Becoming a Soccer Mom	Definition After Becoming a Soccer Mom
post	common name for a newspaper, as in *New York Post* or *Washington Post*	eight-foot-high vertical support for the goal net; close but unsuccessful shots sometimes hit the post
red card	heart or diamond	card displayed by referee to indicate he is expelling a player from the match
right back	what you'll be as soon as you're finished going to the bathroom	defensive player to the right of the sweeper
shoot-out	gun fight in a western movie	means of deciding a tie game in Major League Soccer, the top U.S. professional league
soccer	term used by little boys about their sisters, as in, "I'm gonna sock her!"	world's most popular (and time consuming) sport
stopper	small rubber object used to block a sink drain	central defender who plays in front of the sweeper
striker	worker who walks off job over pay or contract dispute	offensive player usually positioned closest to opponent's goal and expected to score the most goals
sweep-er	person who uses broom to sweep the floor	player stationed in front of goalie as next-to-last line of defense

Term	Definition Before Becoming a Soccer Mom	Definition After Becoming a Soccer Mom
tackle	action in American football where a defender wraps his arms around the ballcarrier's body or legs to force him to the ground	action in soccer where a defender slides legs first into the ball to knock it away from the offensive player; often results in a foul if the defender misses the ball and kicks or trips the offensive player
throw-in	extra item included as inducement to close a sale (for example, "I got the serving tray as a throw-in when I bought the antique dishes.")	play that restarts the game after the ball goes out of bounds along the touchline
touch-line	point beyond which teen-age daughter is instructed to slap roving hand of date	sideline of soccer pitch
wall	what convicts in prison movies are always plotting to get over	two or more players lined up shoulder-to-shoulder, 10 yards from the ball, seeking to block an opponent's free kick on goal after a foul; visually distinguished by players using hands to protect vital body parts

Term	Definition Before Becoming a Soccer Mom	Definition After Becoming a Soccer Mom
whiff	brief smell of an odor	totally miss the ball in attempting a kick
wing	part of bird or airplane that enables flight	midfielder positioned to side of field for long thrusts into opponent's territory

you idiot	term used to address motorist about to sideswipe your car	term used to address referee who doesn't call vicious foul committed against your child

Final Exam

I. A player is offside if:

A   he is even with the last defender other than the goalie when his teammate passes him the ball.

B   as soon as the ball is kicked by a teammate, she crosses the midfield line behind all the defenders except the goalie.

C   he is in an offside position near the left sideline when the ball is passed to a teammate near the right sideline.

D   the assistant referee and referee say he is.

II. If your 15-year-old striker is brushed from behind by a defender and falls to the ground clutching his leg in agony, you should:

A   run on the field to his assistance.

B   stay off the field but dial 911 on your cellular phone.

C   yell at him to get up and shake it off.

D   applaud when he finally gets up and make a note to check out the drama program at his high school.

III. The number of pairs of soccer shoes a player needs is:

A   one, which is sufficient for all outdoor purposes; tennis or running shoes are okay for indoors.

B   two: one for outdoor and one for indoor play.

C   three: one for indoor, molded cleats for hard out-door fields, and screw-in cleats for soft outdoor fields.

D   one more than he has at the moment.

IV. The best time to criticize your player's on-field performance is

A   immediately after the mistake is made, when the player will know exactly what you are yelling about from the sideline.

B   at the field as soon as the game is over, so his teammates can also benefit from your expertise.

C   on the drive home from the game, when you can deal with all her shortcomings at once and she has to listen or else walk home.

D   when the player asks for your technical advice or the coach solicits your help in coaching the player.

V. The most exciting goal in soccer is one that is scored

A   with a spectacular bicycle kick.

B   with a leaping header off a corner kick.

C   with a twisting, dipping free kick that clears the wall and just gets under the crossbar.

D   by your kid.

Answers: D-D-D-D-Duh

155

About the Authors

Janet Staihar knew nothing about soccer when her first son started playing in the early 1980s. But she has learned plenty through observation, a few arguments with coaches, lots of tournament trips, several sideline crises, and keeping up with a soccer-manic second son. After an early career as a wire service reporter and then political staffer, she became a public and media relations consultant in the Washington D.C. area. She has worked on soccer projects including World Cup '94 events, representing South Korea in its effort to host World Cup 2002, and raising the visibility of D.C. Scores, a trend-setting inner-city program that uses soccer play to boost academics for elementary school children.

Dick Barnes has written about sports since high school. He first saw top-level soccer in 1960 at the Olympics and then at the Spanish League in Madrid. He has managed his son's select team, the Bethesda (MD) Blitz, since 1991. In 1996, he wrote *What? ME Manage the Soccer Team?*, a nationally acclaimed handbook for youth team managers. He is assistant director of Bethesda Soccer Club's annual regional pre-Thanksgiving tournament and has worked on numerous other local, state or national tournament and promotional soccer activities. In addition to writing, he is also a lawyer and soccer consultant in the Washington D.C. area.

SOCCER ZONES

WRITINGS OUT OF AMERICAN SOCCER

Edited by Anne H. Woodworth

with an Introduction by George Vecsey

119 pp.

Twenty-five writers from around the country combine to make this a unique book in U.S. soccer literature today.

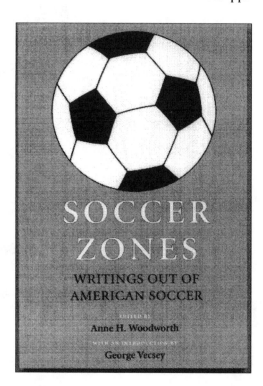

"These are love stories, written by men and women who recognize that kicking a soccer ball is one of the true pleasures in life. . . . They write poems to soccer, they write short stories to soccer, they leave home to play soccer."
—George Vecsey, sports columnist of *The New York Times*, in his Introduction to SOCCER ZONES

"It's a fun read, the American soccer spirit at its best."
—Alexi Lalas, U.S. National Team and Major League Soccer player

ORDER TODAY BY MAIL
See order form on last page of this book

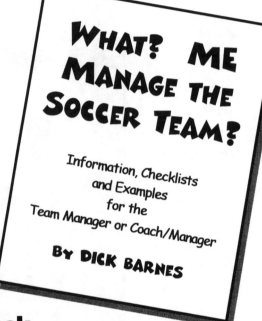

What the news media say about
WHAT? ME MANAGE THE SOCCER TEAM?

First, bookstore shelves filled up with how-to manuals for coaches. Now there are plenty of advice books on parenting youth athletes. Finally, another niche has been addressed: youth soccer team managers.

"What? ME Manage the Soccer Team?: is a handbook for managers of club teams, from the recreational to top select levels. The author is Dick Barnes, a lawyer and journalist who served six years as manager of a Bethesda (Md.) Soccer Club select team.

The book covers a range of logistical tasks, including player registration and arranging tournament trips. But it also helps managers understand who controls youth teams, how to handle dues and budgets, and how to communicate inside and outside the team. Other sections deal with newsletter and field directions; checklists for pre-season, equipment and uniforms, and game-day advice.

Barnes also tackles contentious issues, ranging from playing time and practice attendance to coaches' handling of their own children, and obnoxious sideline conduct by parents.

WASHINGTON SOCCERNET

Area youth club managers — or those soon destined to take over such a position — ought to strongly consider reading Dick Barnes' new handbook, "What? ME Manage the Soccer Team?"

Barnes' publication contains a host of important and useful information to which everyone involved in operating a youth soccer team can turn, whether you're a novice coach forming a U8 team or an experienced manager who thought you knew everything there was to know about running a team properly.

A veteran manager with Bethesda Soccer Club, Barnes covers just about everything in the 52-page booklet, including the basic tasks (registration, tournaments, uniforms, etc.), choosing a tournament, organizing team finances, dealing with contentious issues, and working with your club and leagues.

The Washington Times

Off the press — A new book is apt to help all those soccer moms and dads out there, many of whom may not coach a soccer team but end up being those all-important youth team managers. Dick Barnes has written a handbook called, "What? ME Manage the Soccer Team?" that clearly explains everything a team manager needs to know.

To order, clip or copy this page, fill in, and mail with check or money order to:

Sports Barn Publishing Co.
5335 Wisconsin Ave. NW, Suite 440
Washington DC 20015

Your Order:

Note: If ordering 10 or more books, deduct $1/book and do not include shipping.	. Number Ordered	Total Book Cost	Total Ship'ng Cost
The **Soccer Mom Handbook** $9.95 ea. + $2.00 ea. shipping			
WHAT? ME MANAGE THE SOCCER TEAM? $4.95 ea. + $1.50 ea. shipping			
SOCCER ZONES WRITINGS OUT OF AMERICAN SOCCER $12.95 ea. + $2.00 ea. shipping			
Totals, all books, all shipping			
Sales Tax - 6% of book cost, but only if shipping to address in DC			
Total Due, books + shipping + tax Make check or money order payable to **Sports Barn**			

Send to:

Your Name	
Address	
City	
State ZIP	Phone

Inquire about fund-raising opportunities for your league or club using The Soccer Mom Handbook

Visit us on the internet at http://www.sportsbarn.com